UNCOMMON
KNOWLEDGE

UNCOMMON KNOWLEDGE

The Economist Explains

EXTRAORDINARY THINGS
THAT FEW PEOPLE KNOW

Edited by

TOM STANDAGE

The Economist BOOKS

Published in 2019 under exclusive licence from The Economist by
Profile Books Ltd
29 Cloth Fair
London EC1A 7JQ
www.profilebooks.com

Typeset in Milo by MacGuru Ltd

Printed and bound in Great Britain by CPI Group (UK) Ltd, Croydon CR0 4YY

A CIP catalogue record for this book is available from the British Library

ISBN 978 1 78816 332 3
eISBN 978 1 78283 598 1

Contents

Introduction: The joy of uncommon knowledge

"EVERYTHING THAT IS NEW or uncommon raises a pleasure in the imagination," wrote Joseph Addison, an English essayist and poet, "because it fills the soul with an agreeable surprise, gratifies its curiosity, and gives it an idea of which it was not before possessed." He was writing in 1712, but today, more than three centuries later, his remark neatly summarises the objective of this book.

This is a compendium of explanations, and what they all have in common is that they are uncommon: a word that has two meanings. On the one hand, it refers to things that are rare or infrequently encountered. In the realm of knowledge, that means things that not many people are aware of or know about. But these unusual explanations also have the power to stretch your mind and subtly change how you see the world. In other words, they are uncommon in the second sense of the word, which means exceptional and extraordinary. As Addison observed, uncommon knowledge is enjoyable to encounter because it is unexpected and surprising; because a neat explanation is mentally satisfying; and because encountering a previously unfamiliar idea, and storing it away for future reference, expands the intellect.

Many people would be surprised to hear that the global suicide rate is falling; that most refugees do not live in camps; that carrots were not originally orange; or that the far side of the Moon isn't always dark. They probably couldn't explain why donkey skins are the new ivory; why Westerners are eating so much more chicken; why Americans are sleeping longer than they used to; or why death is getting harder to define. These aren't the sorts of things you wonder about every day. But when you learn the underlying explanations, you do not merely learn something that most people don't know – you also broaden your perspective just a little bit, as your mind makes room for a new way of looking at things. That is the joy of uncommon knowledge, in both senses of the word.

Rooting out these appetising intellectual morsels is something we love to do at *The Economist*, and this book brings together unexpected explanations and fascinating facts from our output of explainers and daily charts. We hope you will enjoy this collection of the fruits of our never-ending quest to uncover the mechanisms that explain why the world is the way it is. By the time you reach the last page, you will have learned things you did not know before – and you will also have equipped your mind to understand the world more fully. Read this book, and you will join the ranks of the uncommonly knowledgeable.

Tom Standage
Deputy Editor, *The Economist*
April 2019

Uncommon knowledge: little-known explanations to stretch your mind

Why Swaziland's king renamed his country

The King of Swaziland, Mswati III, has a problem. "Whenever we go abroad", he says, "people refer to us as Switzerland." So on April 18th 2018, at a celebration marking the 50th anniversary of the country's independence from Britain, the king announced that he was changing Swaziland's name to eSwatini. (As an absolute monarch he can make such decisions.) With its lower-case "e", this new name might seem at first glance to be an attempt to rebrand one of the world's last remaining absolute monarchies as something a little more modern for the internet age. But the new name in fact simply means "Land of the Swazis".

Whether many people did in fact confuse Swaziland with Switzerland is unclear. Both are gorgeous mountainous countries with small populations. Both are landlocked and surrounded by bigger neighbours. But the differences are perhaps more striking. As well as being ruled by a man with 15 wives, Swaziland is a poor country with the highest rate of HIV infection in the world. Some 26% of the adult population is infected. That in turn contributes to a life expectancy at birth of 58 years, the 12th-worst in the world. Changing the name from Swaziland to eSwatini strikes some people as a distraction from bigger issues.

Nonetheless, the king's decision did have a logic to it. Many other former British colonies in Africa took new names on becoming independent. The Gold Coast became Ghana; Northern Rhodesia and Southern Rhodesia became Zambia and Zimbabwe respectively. Basutoland, a tiny enclave surrounded by South Africa, became Lesotho. Swaziland's transformation into eSwatini was much the same story, serving to distance the country from its colonial past, albeit 50 years after the separation. The king had in fact long used the new name in addresses to the United Nations and at the opening of his country's parliament.

But it is likely to take some time to get Swaziland accepted as eSwatini. The Czech Republic is still rarely referred to as "Czechia" in English, despite the best efforts of its government over the past few years to promote the name. In the case of eSwatini, maps and globes will obviously have to be updated, and so will their modern replacements: Google Maps is still using the old name. Within the country, many institutions will have to be renamed. The Royal Swaziland Police, the Swaziland Defence Force, and the University of Swaziland all come to mind. Indeed, the constitution may even have to be rewritten to make sure that the new name sticks.

Why terrorists claim credit for some attacks but not others

Two terrorist attacks hit the southern Philippines in the final days of January 2019. The first, a double bombing at a Roman Catholic church on January 27th, killed at least 20 people. A few days later, an attack on a mosque claimed the lives of two Muslim religious leaders. The jihadists of Islamic State quickly claimed responsibility for the first attack, but the perpetrators of the latter remain unknown.

These attacks were representative of a broader trend. In the past two decades, fewer than half of all terrorist attacks have been either claimed by their perpetrators or convincingly attributed by governments to specific terrorist groups. A paper by Erin Kearns of the University of Alabama, covering 102,914 attacks committed in 160 countries between 1998 and 2016, reveals a consistent pattern to these claims and attributions. Her study shows that attacks causing few deaths, like the assault on the Philippine mosque, tend to remain anonymous. But very deadly ones, such as the attack on a Nepalese military base that killed at least 170 soldiers in 2002, are also less likely than average to be claimed or attributed – particularly when aimed at a military or diplomatic target. Instead, it is those in the middle, causing around 100 deaths, whose perpetrators are most often identified.

What might account for this reverse U-shaped relationship? At one end of the spectrum, terrorist groups have little incentive to claim minor acts of violence. Their opponents could consider such attacks a failure, executed by an incompetent group. At the other extreme, terrorists who inflict the most carnage might fear a backlash from the government or the local population. While killing just a few people may be considered tolerable, extremely savage attacks might threaten the group's survival.

This relationship also holds for attributions by governments. In the absence of fatalities, the state faces less pressure to invest resources into an investigation. After more brutal attacks, a

Blame theory

Global, probability of terrorist attacks being claimed or attributed, 1998–2016, %
By number of fatalities in attack

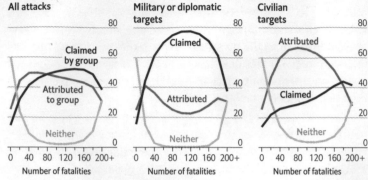

All attacks

Military or diplomatic targets

Civilian targets

Source: "When to take credit for terrorism? A cross-national examination of claims and attributions" by E. M. Kearns, 2019

government has greater incentives to find those responsible – but only up to a point. Attacks on a very large scale are rare, and almost always occur in countries that are poor and authoritarian. Governments in such countries are often less able to investigate attacks, or have no desire to identify the perpetrators.

How carrots became orange

Carrots used to be white. They were grown for their leaves and seeds, much as their distant relatives, parsley and coriander, still are. The chemical compounds that give carrots their vivid colour, carotenoids, are normally used by plants that grow above ground to assist in the process of photosynthesis. But carrots live underground. Subterranean cousins, such as the parsnip and the turnip, are both mainly white. How then did the carrot bring a bit of colour to the dinner table?

Carrots originated in modern-day Iran and Afghanistan. They contain around 32,000 genes (more than humans), of which two recessive ones contribute to a build-up of carotenoids, such as alpha- and beta-carotene. Scientists believe early farmers grew colourful carrots unintentionally, and then continued the practice more purposefully in order to differentiate them from wild ones. Around 1,100 years ago, purple and then yellow varieties emerged, followed another 600 years later, thanks to further selective breeding, by the modern orange form, which has lots of beta-carotene.

There is a theory that orange carrots were promoted by the Dutch, who bred them in honour of William of Orange, the leader of a 17th-century revolt against the Spanish Habsburg monarchy that ruled over a swathe of north-western Europe. Whatever the truth of that particular idea, the orange carrot did become associated with the House of Orange. The conspicuous display of orange carrots at markets came to be seen as a provocative gesture of support for an exiled descendant of William. But whatever their political significance in the past, almost all modern European carrots descend from a variety originally grown in the Dutch town of Hoorn.

The triumph of orange carrots over other varieties ended up being fortuitous. The orange carrot is the most nutritious, and is rich in vitamin A, which contributes to the health of the eye. That spurred another myth, popularised by the British during the second world war, that eating a lot of carrots gives people night-vision. (The story was intended to keep the Royal Air Force's development of radar technology hidden from the Germans, who were encouraged to believe that carrot consumption explained the British pilots' ability to see them coming.) An attempt by a British supermarket to reintroduce the traditional purple variety of carrot in 2002 failed, because shoppers preferred the selectively bred orange sort. The modern preference for orange carrots has led to the breeding of varieties with ever more vivid shades; today's carrots have 50% more carotene than those of 1970. Food for thought.

Why the Mediterranean will eventually disappear

If you happen to find yourself on the Mediterranean Sea, take a minute to observe the shore. Watch closely for a while (for a year, to be precise), and you might notice it move slightly (by about 2cm, or a little less than an inch). Africa and Europe are slowly colliding in a process that has been going on for 40m years, pushing up the Alps and Pyrenees along the way. This continental drift will continue long into the future, until 50m years from now when the two continents meet and become one mega-continent: Eurafrica. The Mediterranean will disappear altogether, to be replaced by a mountain range as big as the Himalayas. It will be an unrecognisable world.

Continental drift is a relatively recent addition to the geological canon, and was only widely accepted in the 1960s. The tectonic plates that underpin the Earth's surface are constantly moving, dragged around by convection currents in the planet's mantle. In recent years, scientists have gained a good understanding of how continents used to move: they now theorise that multiple super-continents have been created in cycles over the course of Earth's history. The most recent such landmass, Pangea, broke up approximately 200m years ago, which means the Earth is currently in the middle of a cycle. Extrapolating from historical data allows researchers to forecast what might be in store.

The next 50m years are relatively easy to predict, and most geologists agree that the Mediterranean will close up. The fate of other seas and oceans is very much up for debate, though. The best-known prediction comes from Christopher Scotese, a geologist at the University of Texas. His "introversion" theory suggests that the Atlantic, which is currently widening, will eventually start to shrink. Over the next 200m years it will slowly close, he suggests, and the Americas will collide with Eurafrica to form Pangea Proxima. Others think the exact opposite could happen: the Atlantic will continue to widen while the Pacific closes, with California eventually colliding with far-east Asia. A frostier forecast holds that all the continents will move north, closing up the Arctic Ocean and forming "Amasia" around the North Pole. A rather different prediction has been proposed by João Duarte at the University of Lisbon. His team think the evidence indicates that both the Atlantic and Pacific Oceans could close. To resolve the spatial conflict that would create, they suggest Asia will cleave in two, being ripped apart along the India/ Pakistan border. A new Pan-Asian ocean would form in the space, becoming the world's largest ocean, while "Aurica" (an assemblage of all the world's existing land masses) would be created in the middle of what was once the Pacific.

Forecasting geological events 200m years ahead is clearly not an exact science. These scientists are in the enviable position of being able to say things that will never be disproved, as it is unlikely that humanity will be around to see the next super-continent form. Nevertheless, such contemplations of the future are rather sobering: a reminder that the land beneath our feet is ultimately little more permanent – on a geological scale – than the borders we draw on its surface.

Why the global suicide rate is falling

Stories about suicide that appear in the news tend to focus on celebrities who have taken their own lives or on clusters of deaths among students. They miss the bigger picture: that, at a global level, suicide has declined by 29% since 2000, and has fallen by 38% from its peak in 1994. Among most Western countries, rates have been falling for decades. In Britain, for instance, the suicide rate peaked in 1934, during the Depression. But elsewhere, the decline has happened more recently. China's rate started to come down in the 1990s; in Russia, Japan, South Korea and India rates have all fallen significantly in the past decade. Western Europe's rate is still declining slowly. America is the big exception: its rate has risen by 18% since 2000. Twenty years ago, America's rate was half China's; now it is twice China's. But looking at the global picture, the net gain is still huge. The drop in the global suicide rate saved 2.8m lives between 2000 and 2018 – three times as many as were killed in battle in that period.

There is no single reason for the global decline, but it is particularly notable among three sets of people. One is young women in China and India. In most of the world, older people kill themselves more often than the young, and men more often than women. But in China and India, young women have been unusually prone to suicide. That is decreasingly the case. The suicide rate among young Chinese women has dropped by 90% since the mid-1990s. Another group is middle-aged men in Russia. After the collapse of the Soviet Union, rates of alcoholism and suicide rocketed among them. Both have now receded. A third category is old people all around the world. The suicide rate among the elderly remains, on average, higher than that among the rest of the population, but it has also fallen faster than among other groups since 2000.

Social change is partly responsible for the falling numbers. Asian women have more freedom and opportunity than before, and, thanks to urbanisation, fewer have access to the highly toxic

Staying alive
Suicides* per 100,000 people

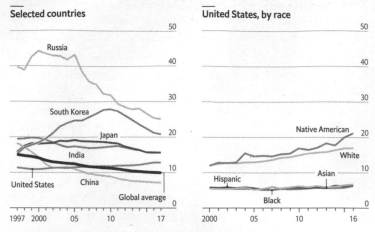

Selected countries

United States, by race

Sources: Institute for Health Metrics and Evaluation; Centres for Disease Control and Prevention   *Age-standardised

pesticides that were once this group's favoured means of suicide. Social stability has returned to Russia and unemployment has fallen. Among the old, poverty has declined at a global level faster than among younger people. Social change may also be partly responsible for the rise in America: suicide has risen most among middle-aged, white, poorly educated rural people – the victims of the "deaths of despair" identified by Anne Case and Sir Angus Deaton, two economists at Princeton University.

Policy also plays a role. When Mikhail Gorbachev introduced restrictions on alcohol in the Soviet Union in 1985, consumption and suicide both plunged; something similar has happened since Vladimir Putin introduced new rules in 2005. Restricting access to easy means to kill oneself can make a big difference because suicide is a surprisingly impulsive act. Of 515 people who survived the leap from San Francisco's Golden Gate Bridge between 1937 and 1971, 94% were still alive in 1978 – which suggests that a suicide postponed is likely to be a suicide prevented. The banning of toxic pesticides has had a clear impact on rates in countries such as South Korea and Sri Lanka. Selling paracetamol and aspirin in only very small quantities has also been shown to reduce suicides. Investing in health services (particularly palliative care, which helps make life tolerable for the chronically sick) can make a difference too. And if America restricted gun ownership, suicide rates would almost certainly crash. America's rate is twice that in Britain (which has tight gun controls). Half of America's suicides are by firearm. And the difference in suicide rates between states – which range from 26 per 100,000 people each year in Montana to five in Washington, DC – is largely explained by variations in levels of gun ownership.

Who owns what in space

In 2015 America's Congress passed a law to legalise mining in outer space – the first of its kind in the world. Firms that someday manage to mine asteroids for resources like water or precious metals would henceforth be allowed to own, process and sell anything harvested. The nascent space-mining industry was thrilled. The boss of a company called Planetary Resources compared it to the Homestead Act of 1862 – a law that gave up to 160 acres in the American West to any plucky settler willing to venture forth. More recently Wilbur Ross, the commerce secretary, has talked about creating a more "permissive" regulatory environment in space and turning the Moon into a "gas station" for further exploration. Other countries have followed suit: Luxembourg passed a similar measure in 2017 and earmarked €200m to invest in space-mining companies. But not everyone is pleased. At a UN committee dealing with outer space, Russia condemned the American move, citing America's "total disrespect" for international law. Critics say America is conferring rights that it has no authority to confer. There are indeed legal grey areas. So who owns what in outer space?

Space is a commons. That was determined in the 1950s by a UN committee, and laid out a decade later in the Outer Space Treaty. No country can lay claim to the Moon, asteroids or other celestial bodies; space is open to all for exploration. The language of early treaties is notably grand, with space referred to as the "province of all mankind". Reality has been far more fraught. In 1957 the Soviet Union launched Sputnik, Earth's first artificial satellite. The achievement heightened American anxieties that nuclear tensions could spill over and upwards. Both countries determined to protect outer space from nuclear confrontation by enshrining the principle of peaceful use.

A nuclear standoff in space is no longer the foremost concern. At issue now is commercial activity, as private companies – rather than nation-states – look to space for profit. Developed in the 1950s and 1960s, space law is state-centric and arguably ill-suited to a commercial future. The legal status of resources mined in space remains ambiguous, and industry wants clarification. The laws adopted by America and Luxembourg were first steps in that direction. But national law will only protect firms from competing claims by their compatriots, notes Tanja Masson-Zwaan, a space-law expert. A Chinese company will not be bound by American law. "It's in everybody's interest to have some kind of international governance system," she adds. One analogy is the high seas, where the International Seabed Authority grants licences for drilling. Another less likely model is Antarctica, where mining was banned under international agreement for 50 years, from 1998.

Does any of this matter? The market for asteroid minerals is currently non-existent. But that is likely to change, as technical hurdles diminish and commercial activity – such as space tourism – develops. One idea is to extract water from asteroids and break it down into hydrogen and oxygen to refuel rockets in space. That would be far cheaper than transporting fuel from Earth and would permit longer flights with heavier payloads. Asteroid mining looks to be at least decades away, but expect a land grab when it comes.

Why most refugees do not live in camps

There are more refugees than at any time since the second world war. The UN Refugee Agency estimated in 2018 that 66m people worldwide had been forcibly displaced from their homes. Of these, 23m are refugees – people who have fled their home country. Across the world, giant camps have sprung up to accommodate them, including Zaatari in Jordan, Dadaab in Kenya and Kutupalong in Bangladesh. These sprawling tent cities are what most people picture when they think of refugees. But most refugees do not live in camps. Why is this, and where do they live instead?

Camps make it easier to take care of refugees, largely by concentrating them all in one place. Host governments and aid agencies can quickly build tents for housing, distribute food rations and set up clinics and schools. Refugees in camps are wonderfully easy to inoculate. Camps can swiftly expand to cope with a sudden surge of new arrivals. Many governments also like to keep refugees in a place where they can easily be counted, registered, screened to make sure they are not terrorists, and cordoned off from the local population.

But life in a refugee camp is often miserable. Many such camps are in remote places. Residents usually struggle to find work, and become dependent on handouts. Many countries ban refugees from working at all. The worst camps can feel like prisons. Refugees are sometimes prevented from leaving. In Iraq's semi-autonomous Kurdistan region, for instance, thousands of Arabs fleeing areas controlled by Islamic State in 2015 were detained in camps and barred from returning home while Kurdish authorities screened them for links to the jihadists. Camps are often crowded, especially in places where lots of refugees have arrived all at once. Some host governments see camps as temporary and do not want camp-dwellers to get too comfortable. Bangladeshi authorities were reluctant to allow the construction of shelters of brick or concrete in camps for Rohingyas fleeing persecution in Myanmar, even though the plastic tents they live in are far more vulnerable to monsoon flooding.

Most refugees therefore avoid camps. The UN estimates that 69% opt instead to live in towns and cities. The better-off rent apartments; others stay with family or friends. The poorest live on the streets. It is harder to access aid outside a camp, but much easier to find a job. Even informal and ill-paid work (the most common sort) is often preferable to the indignity, confinement and squalor of a camp. A startling 80% of refugees have been displaced for ten or more years, according to the International Rescue Committee, a non-profit organisation. Small wonder they quit camps and move to cities, where they have a better chance of rebuilding their lives. Aid agencies are gradually adapting to this reality. The UN Refugee Agency issued new policy guidance in 2014, emphasising that camps should only be temporary and urging that refugees should be integrated into their host communities whenever possible. Many NGOs are exploring new ways of distributing aid in cities, including giving refugees cash to shop in local markets, or providing support to local families that host displaced people. To those who complain that refugee camps are a burden on the host country, the answer is clear: let the refugees out of the camps, and let them work.

Why most countries drive on the right side of the road

In the lead-up to Högertrafikomläggningen, or Day H, Sweden's traffic planners were hard at work. They spent weeks drawing up new intersections and revising one-way systems; workers laboured to add new doors to the other side of thousands of buses. The night before, road markings were hastily repainted, bus stops moved and some 360,000 street signs rejigged. Then, following a national countdown on the radio, at 5am on September 3rd 1967, Swedish motorists switched from the left- to the right-hand side of the road. Despite public opposition, the switch made sense. Most Swedes owned cars with steering wheels on the left, and drivers positioned on the outside of the road caused lots of accidents when overtaking. Collisions were particularly common near Sweden's borders with its neighbours, who all drove on the other side. By switching to the right, Sweden became the last country in continental Europe to conform to a rule now followed by almost three-quarters of countries. How do countries decide which side of the road to drive on?

Driving on the right was not always the norm. Throughout the Middle Ages, traffic tended to stick to the left (though this was more a general rule-of-thumb than enforced regulation). Even before that, Roman soldiers marched on the left-hand side. Historians are not entirely sure why. Many think this was because it suited swordsmen, the majority of whom were right-handed. Being on the left, the thinking goes, meant that when they drew their weapons, their sword-wielding arm would be in the middle of the road and could therefore best strike oncoming foes. Peter Norton from the University of Virginia, however, describes this idea as pure speculation and puts the habit down to chance. Swordsmen were perfectly capable of crossing to the other side of road to have a sword fight, he says.

Things started to change in parts of North America in the late 18th century. One theory puts this down to more big wagons trundling up and down roads. These wagons, pulled by multiple pairs of horses, had no seats. The driver sat on the horse on the left of the rearmost pair so that his whip could reach every animal and, historians speculate, consequently preferred to drive on the right in order to be able to see oncoming traffic clearly by looking down the centre of the road. At around the same time, travelling on the right caught on in revolutionary France, where the side of road people travelled on carried class connotations. The poor generally stuck to the right to allow aristocrats to travel on the left. After the revolution, those aristocrats who had retained possession of their heads switched to the right to avoid sticking out. In 1794 Robespierre made it official with an order that all traffic in Paris stick to the right. Later, as Napoleon, an enthusiastic rule-maker, swept through Europe, he switched the countries he conquered to the right-hand side. Indeed, areas which avoided Napoleon's clutches generally stayed on the left. That includes what became Czechoslovakia, which was only forced to switch to the right by Hitler in 1939. Colonial powers acted similarly, subjecting their domains to their traffic rules.

The tendency towards driving on the right was cemented in the 1920s with the advent of motor cars and accompanying standardisation. Countries with mixed systems, such as Canada, settled on the right because their neighbours were already driving on that side. The tilt to the right accelerated with decolonisation in the 1960s. Once a big country switched, its neighbours generally followed suit. After Nigeria changed to drive on the right in 1972, for instance, the pressure grew on Ghana, the last remaining country in west Africa still sticking to the left. It switched two years later. A similar pattern occurred in the Arab world. Islands such as Britain and Japan, by contrast, have held out and stayed on the left. Most of the 58 countries that drive on the left side of the road are former British colonies or their neighbours. Might any of them be lured to the right? It seems unlikely, considering the higher costs that would be involved compared with last century, when traffic was lighter. The last country to switch was Samoa, in 2009, which went the other way, swapping right for left to match relatively nearby Australia and New Zealand.

How domestic violence affects the economy

The toll of domestic violence is physical and psychological, but it is also economic. Many victims miss work or show up late. Sometimes they (rightly) fear being stalked or killed at their offices. In July 2018 New Zealand passed a law giving victims of domestic violence the right to take ten days' paid leave from work. The goal of the law is to allow people to attend to emergency logistics – moving house, seeking legal help or changing their contact information – without fear of losing their jobs. That is one example of how domestic violence is an economic as well as a social problem.

New Zealand's law has few precedents. The Philippines is the only other country with paid domestic-violence leave, which it enshrined in law in 2004. But a survey in 2015 found that just 39% of Filipino respondents were aware that the law existed, and 26% reported employers reacting negatively to being asked for the leave. Canada offers paid domestic-violence leave in several provinces but not at the national level. Australia's Council of Trade Unions pushed for similar measures in 2017, but had to be satisfied with only five days' unpaid leave. That New Zealand's provision is paid makes a big difference. Research by Women's Refuge, a charity in New Zealand, found that 60% of people had full-time jobs when their abusive relationships began but half of them were no longer employed as those relationships progressed. Many victims stay with abusive partners in part for financial security.

Having passed quite narrowly – by 63 votes to 57 – New Zealand's law is controversial. Victims will not be required to prove that they were abused. Employers, not the government, will pay for their time off. One MP warned the measure might discourage employers from hiring "someone that may present a risk around domestic violence [sic]". In the absence of data, a proxy can be found across the Tasman Sea: the Australia Institute estimates that only a small number – 1.5% of women and 0.3% of men – would use such a law if it were passed in Australia, amounting to A$80m–120m ($59m–89m) a year nationally. But domestic violence itself costs much more. Around the world the cost of violence against women, taking into consideration direct spending on counselling and health resources as well as projections of lost productivity, adds up to 2% of global GDP. In New Zealand, which has one of the highest rates of domestic violence in the developed world, the cost is $2.7bn–4.7bn.

Passing a law to protect the victims of domestic abuse will not prevent violence. New Zealand promoted its law with a government-sponsored public campaign. Advocates caution that such laws need to be combined with training for employers. Whether companies can and are willing to pay up will be watched closely as the policy takes effect. If well implemented, it could provide an economic safety net for women as they deal with traumatic situations. As Jan Logie, the politician who proposed the bill, said, "It doesn't make sense to tell victims we want them to leave, and then force them into poverty when they do."

Why school summer holidays are too long

It's a July day in the Welsh town of Barry, and the adults walking out of the primary school look visibly relieved. They have just dropped their children off at a summer programme, which provides meals and activities for the day. Mere days into the six-week summer holidays, these parents say they are already struggling to keep their children entertained, and wish the break were shorter. Many experts would agree, arguing that the long break harms children. Why do they believe summer holidays are too long, and what should be done instead?

The vast majority of the world's school calendars have long summer holidays, their length ranging from three weeks in South Korea to three months in America, Italy and Turkey. The holidays' 19th-century origins are hazy. They are popularly believed to be a hangover from the West's agrarian past, when families needed their children's help in the fields during the summer, though many historians think the evidence for this is thin. In the popular imagination, school summer holidays conjure up a picture of carefree youthful exploration. But for many children and their families, the reality is very different.

Research, mostly from America, suggests that children will return from the long break having forgotten much of what they were taught the previous year. One study from an unnamed state in the American South found that this "summer learning loss" could equate to a quarter of the year's education. Poor children tend to be the worst affected: a study carried out in 2007 in Baltimore found that variations in summer loss might account for two-thirds of the achievement gap between rich and poor children by the age of 14 or 15. Evidence from outside America is more scarce. But studies have found that children also regress over the summer break in Belgium, Britain, Canada, Germany and Malawi, all of which have much shorter holidays than America. For parents too, summer holidays can be challenging. Many rely on the term-time services that schools provide for their offspring, such as supervision and meals.

Come the holidays, parents can suddenly find their schedules and budgets stretched.

Experts suggest three types of solutions to the problems posed by the long summer holidays: extending school years, spreading holidays to other times of the year, and more state provision of summer-holiday activities. Advocates for the first approach point enviously to South Korea, which has the world's longest school year and the shortest summer break. South Korean students score brilliantly on comparative measures such as the OECD's PISA (international student assessment) test of maths, science and reading skills. But there is a cost: they also have a higher incidence of mental-health problems than children in other rich countries. What of spreading holidays more evenly through the school year? Some experts say there is little public support for restructuring the school calendar, which is often deeply ingrained in tradition, and that the evidence (albeit limited) on year-round schooling remains inconclusive. So that leaves increased funding for summer activities. This may allow children to develop skills not emphasised in the school curriculum. "We need more learning [over the summer]," says Matthew Boulay of the National Summer Learning Association, an American NGO, "but not necessarily more schooling."

Where people most want to emigrate to

In December 2018, 164 members of the United Nations adopted the Global Compact for Safe, Orderly and Regular Migration. The 34-page document is not legally binding, but it encourages governments to treat immigrants humanely, inform them of their rights and welcome them into society. President Donald Trump withdrew the United States from negotiations on the compact in 2017. Explaining this decision, his ambassador to the UN said that decisions about American immigration policy "must always be made by Americans and Americans alone".

Until July 2018, when the final draft of the compact was published, America was the only one of the UN's 193 members to have boycotted it. But other governments then followed Mr Trump's lead. The list of countries that have refused to take part includes a few rich countries that are preoccupied with strong borders (such as Australia, Switzerland and Israel) and several eastern European countries whose people are sceptical about immigration (such as Hungary, the Czech Republic and Bulgaria).

The compact is far from perfect. It is vague about how countries should co-operate on many issues, such as border management and access to public services. It offers no radical solutions for making immigration more palatable to locals (such as an additional tax on immigrant incomes, which might form part of a broader deal to allow more migration). But it lays out some sensible ground rules: ensuring that all migrants and refugees carry some sort of identification; requiring them to communicate their entry requirements and document their skills; and keeping them out of detention centres if possible. Above all, the compact asserts that the best way for governments to improve control over their borders is for them to work together.

Interestingly, the American president's scorn for migrants and globalism has not dampened the global appeal of migrating to America. Gallup, a pollster, has found that given the chance, 158m people worldwide would move permanently to the United States

Chasing the American dream

Countries to which people want to migrate	Countries most welcoming to immigrants
Potential immigrants, m	Acceptance index, 9=best

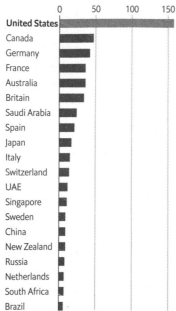

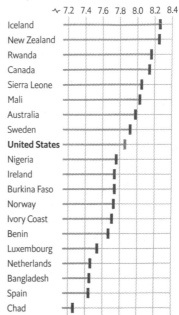

Source: Gallup

– and that the share of would-be migrants who pick the country as their first choice has remained roughly constant since 2010. Moreover, despite Mr Trump's rhetoric, Americans seem to be becoming friendlier to foreigners. In 2018 Gallup reported that a record 75% of Americans think immigration is good for the country, up from 66% in 2012. On the pollster's migration acceptance index, which measures how comfortable people are with foreign neighbours or in-laws, America ranks ninth in the world. The Trump administration is unlikely to change its mind. But if the upward trend in migrant acceptance continues, then it is possible to imagine a future president signing up to the UN's accord.

Globally curious: particular proclivities from around the world

Why Australians are divided over kangaroos

Australians are not, as they sometimes joke, the only people to eat their iconic national animal. Swedes munch on moose; in Spain, bull-tail stew is a delicacy. But the culling of kangaroos divides opinion Down Under. Many view the marsupials as pests that destroy pasture and cause clashes by hopping in front of cars. Animal-rights types counter that killing them is inhumane, and that kangaroo meat is rife with bacteria.

Annual aerial surveys suggest that there are more than 47m kangaroos bounding through the outback, making them some of the most populous large vertebrates on earth. Their natural predators, such as dingoes, are scarce, so when the vegetation they eat is abundant, their numbers jump. State governments have long set "harvesting" quotas to keep the four most populous species in check. But some ecologists suggest that the population estimates are over-optimistic, and that the culls are damaging.

Those in favour of culling point out that Australia earns $175m annually from the carcasses, which are butchered in struggling rural towns. Some scientists argue that kangaroos are a more sustainable source of protein than cows or sheep. Yet the industry is under pressure abroad. Cuddly campaigns have turned shoemakers such as Adidas against kangaroo leather and sapped foreign appetite for kangaroo meat. In 2016 California reinstated an embargo on kangaroo products.

As a result, professional hunters receive a lower price for every carcass they deliver. They killed 1.4m kangaroos in 2016, a fifth of the permitted maximum. But a higher kangaroo population simply means that more will die in the next drought, says George Wilson of the Australian National University. Worse, he says, if skilled hunters lay down their arms, rookies will take over. In Queensland, landholders have been accused of poisoning kangaroos and erecting fences to prevent them from reaching water. The back and forth is endless.

Why is Finland so happy?

In the 1860s Finland suffered a famine that killed about 9% of its population. It has come a long way since. In March 2018 Finland was named the happiest country in the world by the UN's Sustainable Development Solutions Network. Three of its Nordic cousins, Norway, Denmark and Iceland, took the next consecutive places. Finns can boast of myriad other number-one spots. In recent years their country has been named the most stable, the freest and the safest by various organisations. These accolades may be understandable; but in a country where temperatures regularly hover around -20°C and some parts hardly get any sunlight for a big chunk of the year, what do the locals have to be so happy about?

The World Happiness Report, as the survey was called, used global polling data from Gallup to measure how pleased people felt with their lives. The researchers then tried to explain the differences using variables such as GDP per person, social support, healthy-life expectancy, freedom to make life choices, generosity and freedom from corruption. The differences between top-ranking countries are tiny, and the top five have not changed for years. This year's report measured immigrant happiness for the first time, and Finland topped this category as well. This suggests that happy societies are those with supportive social systems and institutions that make it harder for people to fall through the cracks. They are also more willing to accept and integrate immigrants. Unsurprisingly, the poorest and most violent countries were the most miserable – there is little to celebrate in war-torn Yemen or Syria.

The secret to Finland's happiness might just be how boring it is. A Finnish saying sums it up well: "Happiness is having your own red summer cottage and a potato field." Free education, generous parental leave and a healthy work-life balance ensure that people have the time and the means to pursue their pleasures, no matter how mundane. Over 80% of Finns trust the country's police, education and health-care systems. And because of progressive taxation and wealth redistribution, the lifestyles of the rich and the poor are not dramatically divergent. Neither are those of men and women. Finland is widely considered one of the best places in the world to be a mother, and to be a working woman. Though suicide rates are distressingly high, Finland has reduced these by 30% since 2000. The happiness of immigrants stems from a strong support network and integration policies, but also from the fact that immigrants in Finland tend to come from places that are culturally close, like neighbouring Estonia and Russia.

The happiness rankings contain some surprises. The happiest countries are not necessarily the richest. Though America has doubled its income per person in the past 40 years, this seems not to have increased the subjective well-being of its people. It slipped to 18th place, five rungs down from 2016. Britain came in 19th. The researchers cite obesity, depression and opioid addiction as some of the factors dragging down rich countries. What is more, people of different ages, cultures and social classes define joy in different ways. People in Latin America reported they were significantly happier than their countries' wealth, corruption or high levels of violence would suggest, because their happiness is connected to strong family bonds. And other cultural factors and national characteristics may also play a part. The Finns have a word, *sisu*, which means stoic perseverance and grit – in the face of whatever comes your way.

Why universities for the elderly are booming in China

Several times a year, groups of silver-haired Chinese people camp out overnight. They do so in order to get prime spots to register for places at the country's universities for the elderly. Since 1983, when China's first such school opened, 70,000 more have cropped up across the country. They offer courses in pursuits like dancing, online shopping or English for would-be travellers, as well as in more traditional academic disciplines. In 2017 these universities enrolled a combined 8m students – just over 3% of China's cohort of over-60s. At the Shanghai University for the Elderly, the average age of students is between 65 and 70.

The idea of a university for the elderly is not new. The University of the Third Age movement, named for the final third of life, began in France in 1973. It then spread across Europe and became especially popular in Britain. China's first universities for the elderly were aimed at veteran Communist Party cadres. Today some of the schools are reserved for retired civil servants, but others are open to all. Most are government-funded; the average cost of fees is 200 yuan ($31) per term.

Demand is high and will only grow. In Shanghai, one in every six interested students is able to enrol; in Hangzhou, it is just one in 16. Several schools have adopted lottery systems; others are first-come, first-served. The number of Chinese people aged 60 and over is projected to increase from 241m to 487m, or almost 35% of all Chinese citizens, by 2050. China has the world's fastest-ageing population. The one-child-per-couple policy – which was in place from 1979 to 2016 – contributed to this demographic imbalance. It resulted in the "4-2-1 phenomenon", which sees one child trying to look after two parents and four grandparents.

The government aims to have one university for the elderly in every county by 2020. After all, educating seniors makes practical sense: it helps to improve memory and to fight loneliness, which damages health and drives up suicide rates. It is also in line with

Confucian thought, which teaches that learning is a lifelong virtue. But these schools will not fix all the difficulties caused by China's ageing population. They are no replacement for formal medical care, especially for poor Chinese. They do not address the government's astronomical social-security bill. And they do not make up for a labour shortage. To do that, the government has considered raising the retirement age (which is 55 or 50 for women, depending on the industry, and 60 for men). In the meantime, senior students have taken heart from Mao Zedong's idiom: "Study hard and every day you will improve."

Why India avoids alliances

As China grows in economic power and military might, other Asian players are looking to India as a likely counterweight. Their thinking is that with its population set to overtake China's in the next decade and its economy growing faster, India will be uniquely equipped to stand up to the region's potential bully. That is why big powers such as America and Japan, along with smaller ones such as Australia, Singapore and France (which has island territories in the Indian and Pacific Oceans), have been courting India as an ally with growing urgency. Yet much as it sympathises with fellow democracies and harbours its own deep concerns about China, India keeps brushing them off. Prime Minister Narendra Modi has worked hard to cultivate personal ties with President Xi Jinping; in April 2018 the two held an informal two-day summit in Wuhan. India's biggest arms-supplier is Russia, an increasingly close ally of China. Some in Delhi even counsel shunning the West and seeking a similar alliance with neighbours to the north. Why is India so aloof?

To countries worried by the rise of China, the construction of a containing ring of military allies looks sensible. Individually, small Asian countries are no match for the Chinese dragon; allied with bigger powers, they might be. An obvious missing piece of the ring is India. This seems strange. India has plenty of reasons to be wary of China. The two fought a brief border war in 1962; each still claims territories the other holds, and this remains a cause of periodic scuffling. China props up India's nuclear-armed rival Pakistan with generous doses of arms and money; it has made increasingly bold inroads in smaller countries that India views as part of its own traditional sphere of influence, such as the Maldives, Nepal and Sri Lanka. Another annoyance is that China also runs a big and growing trade surplus with India. Partly in response to all this, India has warmed to America in recent years, signing small-scale military co-operation agreements and contracts for some American arms. It also sustains cordial military ties with regional democracies that would love a deeper strategic engagement. But even so, India has consistently shied away from formalising such relationships into anything resembling an alliance.

Frustrated Western suitors tend to interpret such prevarication as a lack of political will. But Indian dithering is less hapless than it may seem. Since its birth as a nation in 1947, India has consistently sought – though not always convincingly achieved – full strategic autonomy. During the cold war it was far enough from the important theatres of Soviet-American rivalry to avoid taking sides. As Indian leaders then dabbled with socialism, explored friendships with other post-colonial states and saw America pumping arms into Pakistan as a reward for its ruling generals' "anti-Communism", they grew disillusioned with the West. India was one of the founders of the Non-Aligned Movement that sought to form a third pole amid East-West rivalries. It abhorred America's involvement in Vietnam, and in 1971 was shocked by the Nixon administration's fierce opposition to independence for Bangladesh. Later, India opposed brash American policies, such as the 2003 invasion of Iraq. It also resented being punished for developing nuclear weapons even as China, which tested its atom bomb just ten years before India, was welcomed into the nuclear club. Only in the past decade has America distanced itself from Pakistan, and tried more actively to woo India.

So, although India is indeed wary of China, it also bears a legacy of mistrust towards America. India's establishment instinctively prefers the West, but its strategic thinkers caution that the country should avoid entangling alliances. Vast oceans separate countries such as America and Australia from China, they note, but with India it shares a long land border. China's economy is now five times the size of India's, so it would be rather risky to signal to such a neighbour that India favours a "containment" strategy. Besides, India has a strong sense of itself as an emerging superpower. Until now, in the modern world, an underperforming economy has held it back from playing a bigger role. Given time and patience, though, India itself will become a powerful pole in a multipolar world.

How California could split up

California's boundaries were established in 1849, paving the way for it to join the United States the following year. Its admission to the union as a free state was one of many compromises made before the civil war between the states that allowed slavery and those that did not. At the time, much of California was considered uninhabitable, compared with lands further east. It was full of mountains, forests and river valleys that routinely flooded. The state census of 1850 counted fewer than 100,000 people. Now, 170 years later, the state is America's most populous and wealthiest by some distance, with 40m residents and the world's fifth-largest economy. Some consider it too big and too unwieldy, and various movements are pursuing dreams of breaking it up.

The notion of carving up a state is not new. Proposals for splitting California date back to 1855. And the desire for change is not unique to California. In 2011 Democrats in Pima County, Arizona, proposed turning their 1m-person county into "Baja Arizona". Two years later, 11 counties in northern Colorado, where three in four voters had chosen Mitt Romney for president, voted on whether to take their oil and gas deposits and create a sparsely populated new state. Neither group made much progress. In California, rural and urban areas can have very different attitudes to taxation, spending, gun licensing and the exploitation of public lands. With some exceptions, the less-populated parts of California lean towards conservatism, whereas the urban ones, which enjoy much of the employment and the wealth, lean Democratic. The so-called Big Sort – the name given by Bill Bishop, an American journalist, to the phenomenon of Americans increasingly moving to live near those who share their political views – happens at an appropriately large scale in California: big cities are heavily liberal, while rural counties have grown more conservative.

The proposed splits of the state tend to emphasise the effects of the sorting process. The New California proposal, which paints the state government as a den of tax-crazed socialists, would carve out mainly rural counties into a 51st state. By contrast, Tim Draper, a billionaire, argues that California is simply too big for good governance, and that smaller states would serve residents better, though he has stated no specific policy or taxation goals. He once proposed a six-way split, but now favours three states: NorCal would encompass San Francisco and northern California; Cal would grab most of the rest of the coast, including Los Angeles; and SoCal would occupy San Diego and the once-fertile Inland Empire and the southern Central Valley.

Impediments to such changes abound. The last splitting of a state took place in 1863, when parts of Virginia, a Confederate state, became the Union state of West Virginia. For a state to splinter, both chambers of the state legislature would have to approve a resolution, and so would the House and Senate in Washington, DC. Mr Draper says a citizen's initiative would allow his scheme to bypass the state legislature. But even if approved by a majority of Californians, the matter would almost certainly be contested on constitutional and procedural grounds. And even if a successful initiative's validity were upheld, Congress is unlikely to vote to increase California's senatorial delegation. But another approach has been put forward. Calexit, a secession proposal by the Yes California group, would keep the state whole – as an independent country. But the group had to abandon an attempt to get a vote for its scheme on the ballot, after its co-founder was discovered to have relocated to Russia. So California seems unlikely to split up, or split off, any time soon.

Why Delhi wants to become a state

In July 2018 the Indian Supreme Court issued a sharp rebuke to the central government. It ruled that Delhi, the country's capital, should be allowed to run its affairs without constant interference from the lieutenant-governor, an appointed official. The judgment ended three years of rising tension and growing paralysis during which Narendra Modi's government and his Bharatiya Janata Party (BJP) had wielded a panoply of instruments, from police to courts to the governor's office, to thwart the city's elected leaders. Despite its court victory, the Aam Aadmi Party, which had been in charge of the city since 2015, demanded further concessions. What lies behind its demand that Delhi should enjoy not just limited self-rule, but the same federal status as India's 29 states?

The trouble with Delhi's city politics can be traced back to soon after India's independence, in 1947. As an administrative centre drawing bureaucrats from across India, and as the sensitive nucleus of government, it was given special status as a National Capital Territory – not unlike Washington, DC, or Brasília. What evolved was a hybrid arrangement. Delhi would have an elected assembly and a chief minister, to give its people a voice. But to preserve the central government's prerogatives, as well as security, the city itself would not control its own land, police or public order. An appointed lieutenant-governor would in theory not interfere with day-to-day affairs, but would see that the city government respected Delhi's primary duty as a seat of national government. It was an uncomfortable arrangement with built-in tensions, but despite Delhi's growth, from just 1.3m people in 1950 to some 20m today (or 26.5m if you count surrounding suburbs), things worked pretty well most of the time. It helped that quite often a single party held power both at the "centre" and in Delhi.

But in 2015 the Aam Aadmi Party, an anti-corruption upstart party, won an unprecedented 67 of 70 seats in the Delhi assembly. The BJP, meanwhile, had won a resounding victory in national elections. Both parties were aggressive and ambitious. Aam Aadmi sought to widen its appeal on the national stage, while the far more powerful BJP aimed to stifle its puny rival at birth. By varied means, such as by asserting the lieutenant-governor's power to hire, fire and transfer Delhi's own administrative workers, the BJP tried to make Aam Aadmi's leaders look unfit to run the city. The resulting clashes left neither party looking good, but it was the city's inhabitants who suffered most from stalled government programmes and a failure to address chronic problems such as severe air pollution. Their exasperation reached a peak in June 2018, when rival sit-ins picketed the governor and the chief minister while the city's most senior (and centrally appointed) civil servants mounted a boycott of Aam Aadmi directives.

The Supreme Court ruling was a moral victory for Aam Aadmi, but the BJP pushed back. Civil servants loyal to the "centre" insisted that they did not need to take orders from the city government. For its part, Aam Aadmi vowed to carry its pitch for statehood to the public, and mount a sustained pressure campaign. After all, it argues, India's map has changed frequently since independence, with popular movements forcing the creation of numerous new states, carved from the original set. Given its population and special needs, Delhi certainly deserves a more fully empowered local government. Its people, however, are far more diverse in origin than those of any existing state. They may not easily unite behind the call for statehood.

How smog affects spending in China

Walk down the street in a Chinese city, and you are likely to see nearly as many *kouzhao* as eyeglasses or wristwatches. Anti-pollution masks that cover the nose and mouth have become ubiquitous on the streets of Beijing and Shanghai, especially during the winter months when coal is burned for heat. Chinese consumers, particularly those living in busy megacities, shell out 4bn yuan ($600m) on masks every year. Many are manufactured in Dadian, a town in Shandong province in eastern China known as "mask village".

Kouzhao may be the most visible expense caused by China's toxic air, but they are far from the largest one. A working paper published in 2018 by America's National Bureau of Economic Research suggests that the costs of pollution in the country may be far greater than previous studies have suggested. Panle Jia Barwick, Shanjun Li, Deyu Rao and Nahim Bin Zahur, a group of economists at Cornell University, analysed the relationship between air pollution and health-care spending across 367 Chinese cities. Combining hourly pollution readings with debit- and credit-card transactions made between 2013 and 2015, they found that when levels of $PM_{2.5}$ (fine-particulate matter) are high, consumers tend to spend more on health-care goods and services. A temporary 10 micrograms per cubic metre ($\mu g/m^3$) jump in $PM_{2.5}$ is associated with an 0.65% surge in health-care transactions. A permanent increase of this magnitude yields an increase of 2.65%, which the authors estimate to be worth 59.6bn yuan ($9.2bn). Although air pollution leads to higher spending at hospitals and pharmacies, it causes spending at supermarkets to fall as shoppers opt to stay indoors.

Such findings suggest that efforts by the government to cut air pollution could yield significant savings. Since 2014, when Li Keqiang, China's premier, declared "war" on air pollution, the country has closed polluting factories, shuttered coal-fired power plants and taken millions of vehicles off the roads. These measures have helped reduce concentrations of $PM_{2.5}$ in major Chinese cities

Get thee to an apothecary
China, consumer spending* in relation to concentration of PM$_{2.5}$, 2013–15

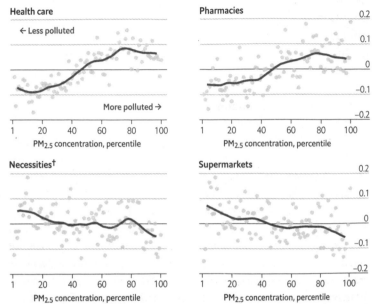

Health care

← Less polluted

More polluted →

1 20 40 60 80 100
PM$_{2.5}$ concentration, percentile

Pharmacies

0.2
0.1
0
−0.1
−0.2

1 20 40 60 80 100
PM$_{2.5}$ concentration, percentile

Necessities[†]

1 20 40 60 80 100
PM$_{2.5}$ concentration, percentile

Supermarkets

0.2
0.1
0
−0.1
−0.2

1 20 40 60 80 100
PM$_{2.5}$ concentration, percentile

Source: "The morbidity cost of air pollution: evidence from consumer spending in China", P. J. Barwick, S. Li, D. Rao and N. Bin Zahur, NBER, 2018

*Number of credit/debit–card transactions (log values) after controlling for holidays, weather, day of the week, etc.
[†]Excluding supermarkets

by 32%. If the country's PM$_{2.5}$ levels were cut to 10 µg/m³, a level deemed safe by the World Health Organisation, the study's authors reckon that Chinese households could save tens of billions of dollars in health-care expenses. That would provide a welcome financial cushion to the vast majority of the country – though the residents of "mask village" might harbour mixed feelings.

How many Americans believe in ghosts?

Surviving winters 2,000 years ago was not easy. In an attempt to increase their chances of survival, Irish pagans would curry favour with evil spirits during the festival of Samhain – which fell at the mid-point between the autumn equinox and the winter solstice – by inviting occupants of the "Otherworld" to feast with them. The tradition persists 2,000 years later, albeit with a distinctively Yankee flavour. Halloween in America is a multi-billion-dollar industry. Each year some 175m Americans spend a total of $9bn dressing up as ghouls, witches and monsters; spraying fake cobwebs over their homes; and wolfing down horror-themed candy.

But what, if anything, remains of the original Gaelic belief that spirits can haunt? On behalf of *The Economist*, YouGov, a pollster, asked a representative sample of American adults whether they believed in ghosts. A shocking 47% of respondents said that they did. Around 15% even said they had seen one.

Suitably spooked, *The Economist* dug a little deeper to find out what factors determine such beliefs. Unsurprisingly, education plays a part. People who left school at 18 or earlier were more likely to believe in ghosts than those who went to college. Age is negatively correlated: the younger people are, the more likely they are to let their imaginations of the afterlife run wild. People who identify as either Middle Eastern, Native American or mixed-race have a higher propensity to believe in ghosts. And faith is instructive, too. Roman Catholics, perhaps because of their veneration of saints, are more likely to believe in ghosts than Protestants. And the more you pray, the more likely you are to believe in the undead.

Most strikingly of all, there is a large gender gap when it comes to belief in the supernatural. Some 53% of women believe in ghosts compared with 40% for men. A similar gender gap persists when respondents are asked whether "people can place curses on other people". That strange gap might have something to do with women being identified as witches – though of the 3,500 people tried for witchcraft in Scotland during the 1600s, about 15% were men.

That's the spirit

Do you believe in ghosts?, United States, % replying* "yes", by demographic group

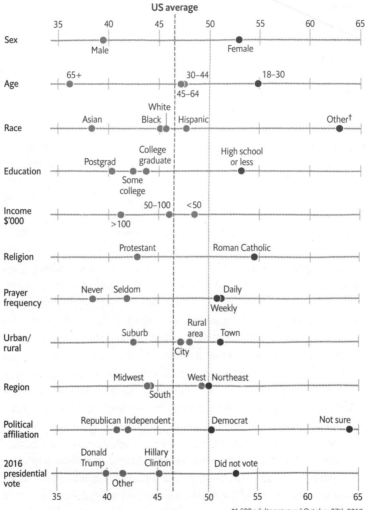

Sources: YouGov; *The Economist*

*1,500 adults surveyed October 27th 2018
†Middle Eastern, Native American and mixed race

Why treason cases are so common in Africa

"Situka!" sings Bobi Wine, a Ugandan singer and politician: "Rise up." With his red beret and fiery lyrics, Mr Wine became one of the most popular opposition figures in Uganda. That evidently riled Yoweri Museveni, the ageing president. In August 2018 Mr Wine was violently arrested. He was later charged with treason, alongside 32 others. Prosecutors claimed that they had thrown stones at the president's convoy. The case rocked the country, but also stirred a sense of *déjà vu*. Opposition politicians have been charged with treason many times before. So have their counterparts in other African countries. Such treason cases are often based on flimsy evidence and rarely lead to convictions (Mr Wine was released a month later). So why do states pursue them?

The obvious reason is to control dissent. Arresting opposition figures gets them off the airwaves and the streets. In some countries, a treason charge makes it impossible to apply for bail. In others the defendants may be bailed – as Mr Wine was – but with restrictions placed on their activities. A tedious succession of hearings can drag on for years. In Zimbabwe under Robert Mugabe treason charges were slapped on opposition figures in the run-up to elections. Elsewhere, they have been used against candidates who question the result. Kizza Besigye, an opposition leader in Uganda, was charged with treason in 2016 after swearing himself in as the "people's president" (he said the official ballot was rigged). And in Kenya, Miguna Miguna, an opposition lawyer with a Canadian passport, was arrested for treason and deported to Canada after overseeing the symbolic swearing-in of the opposition leader Raila Odinga as president in 2018.

Treason is also part of the deeper language of politics. Touchy presidents portray critics as enemies of the state. "Let them demonstrate and they will see who I am," said John Magufuli, the Tanzanian president, in 2018; police declared an unauthorised protest an act of treason. And rulers do not like to be upstaged. Hakainde Hichilema, an opposition leader in Zambia, was arrested for treason in 2017 after his motorcade failed to give way to the president's. Such intolerance has roots in the colonial state. The British locked up nationalist leaders such as Jomo Kenyatta, in Kenya, and Kwame Nkrumah, in Ghana, on a variety of charges. They wrote the law which is now used against Mr Wine.

The space for opposition is especially constrained in countries like Uganda, where the ruling party seized power by force of arms. In such places politics is fought on two fronts. There is the familiar business of arguing on talk shows and campaigning for votes; then there is the real struggle, which is for control of the army and the street. Opposition shades into resistance, which disputes the legitimacy of the regime itself. It is met with force. "The state will kill your children," said the general secretary of the ruling party in Uganda, warning off protests in 2016. Under Mr Museveni, the subtext of all politics in Uganda is violence. Protest looks like rebellion, and opposition like treason, because the state cannot imagine things any other way.

Why Australia loses so many prime ministers

In the quarter of a century to 2007, Australia had three prime ministers. Since then not a single one has survived a full three-year term. First went Kevin Rudd, a Labor leader who was replaced by his deputy, Julia Gillard, in 2010. When her popularity plummeted, he knifed her in return but lost a general election shortly after. That led to the installation of Tony Abbott, a hardline conservative, as prime minister in 2013. But he lasted only until 2015 before being toppled by the more moderate Malcolm Turnbull. In 2018, after a coup fomented by Mr Abbott's hard-right bloc, Mr Turnbull lost his job. Scott Morrison, the former treasurer, became prime minister. That brought the total to six in 11 prosperous years. Why does Australia keep losing leaders?

One reason is that its politicians can replace their bosses in a vote by party MPs known as a leadership "spill". These can happen quickly and brutally, with the winner requiring just 50% of the vote. Spills were rare before this century, so some ascribe their increasing popularity to a modern preoccupation with opinion polls and popularity. Parties often bet that replacing a prime minister will boost support before the next election. A series of weak leaders, nursing personal vendettas, has only added to the problem. (Labor's spills were built on the battle between Mr Rudd and Ms Gillard; among the conservatives, Mr Turnbull and Mr Abbott started attacking each other as early as 2009.) "We've set a precedent," observes Michael Fullilove of the Lowy Institute, a think-tank. "We are waiting for a prime minister who can break it."

Other causes relate to the peculiarities of Australia's parliamentary system. First, its three-year electoral cycle is among the shortest anywhere in the world. Prime ministers have barely been sworn in before parties start thinking about the next election. Second, the Australian senate is one of the world's most powerful. It can neuter governments that do not control it, and not many governments do. The upper house is elected by proportional representation and is dominated by a menagerie of minor parties and independents. Third, it is compulsory to vote in Australia. Ian McCallister, a professor at the Australian National University, estimates that up to 18% of voters take part only because they have to. This cohort is drawn to style over substance, he says, which has underscored a deep culture of personality politics in Australia.

The churn might be easier to understand if Australians were hard done-by. But the economy has not been in recession for 27 years. The coups are increasingly counterproductive. Australians have grown sick of the insecurity they precipitate, and profess historically low trust in their politicians. Support for the Liberals crashed to its lowest level in a decade after the 2018 upheaval. But change is possible. After its back and forth, Labor introduced rules in 2013 that made it harder to knife its leaders. They must now be elected by both MPs and members over a month-long process that is intended to prompt deliberation. Politicians who want to force a spill must deliver a petition signed by 60% of their colleagues. (Liberal rebels, by comparison, still need only half.) Mr Rudd has argued that the change has made it impossible to "launch a coup at the drop of a hat". His successor, Bill Shorten, was unpopular with voters, but survived unchallenged for more than six years. The Liberals might learn something from that.

What is the Northern Sea Route?

On August 23rd 2018 the *Venta Maersk* left the Far-Eastern Russian port of Vladivostok on a journey of great significance. Sailing via the East Siberian and Laptev Seas, and arriving in St Petersburg on September 28th, the *Venta* followed a route that marks the latest development in maritime transport in these northern climes. The specially strengthened vessel was the world's first container ship to venture into the Russian Arctic. Its voyage was only a trial. Its aim was to gather data and determine whether the route is feasible, rather than to seek a commercial alternative to Maersk's existing routes. But experts also interpret the venture in light of growing international interest in the Arctic.

In the past decade melting ice-sheets have opened up previously inaccessible Arctic shipping lanes. China's state-owned shipping company, COSCO, is among the most active players. Since 2013 it has completed more than 30 journeys in the region. And China has poured money into the building of infrastructure along Russia's Arctic coast and into its oil and gas wells there. But for China the Arctic is just one part of a bigger game. The stakes are higher for Russia: 30% of its GDP depends on the region. "Russia's future lies in the Arctic," says Malte Humpert, a senior fellow at the Arctic Institute. "It will become an essential corridor to extract and transport resources to Asia and Europe." And for now Russia can set the rules. After all, it is through its territorial waters that the Arctic's most trafficked shipping lane, the Northern Sea Route (NSR), passes.

The NSR runs from the Barents Sea, near Russia's border with Norway, to the Bering Strait between Siberia and Alaska. Ships sailing through the NSR need the permission of Russian authorities, who collect transit fees and provide escorting icebreakers. The NSR has been touted as a potential rival to the Suez Canal because it could dramatically slash some journey times between Asia and Europe. For example, a ship travelling from South Korea to Germany would take roughly 34 days via the Suez Canal but only 23 days via the NSR. However, the Arctic route has drawbacks: a navigation season of three to four months each year, unpredictable ice conditions, high insurance fees, the need for costly specialised vessels, and a lack of search-and-rescue teams and support infrastructure. These are some of the reasons why experts believe that the NSR will not become an economically feasible alternative before 2040.

Although the NSR might never rival the Suez Canal as the main artery for cargo between Europe and Asia, it could still be important for the shipping of fossil fuels. To be commercially viable, large container ships using the Suez Canal route need to make deliveries to several customers along the way. This business model is unfeasible in the sparsely populated Arctic. But for oil and liquefied-natural-gas tankers, it does make economic sense to serve single markets without intervening stops. The Arctic route is well suited to this kind of shipping. The prospects of the NSR would also improve if the world became less stable. More piracy around the Horn of Africa, more congestion in the Strait of Malacca, more terrorist attacks in the Suez Canal: all would render control of the Northern Sea Route strategically important. Facing little competition from America, Russia and China will have the upper hand.

Resource intensive: oddities and commodities

Why donkey skins are the new ivory

Donkeys are the backbone of many farming villages in developing countries. But if current trends continue, the world's rural poor may soon need to find a new beast of burden. The animals' ranks have thinned dramatically in many African countries: Kenya's donkey population, for example, has fallen by half since 2009, to 900,000. The primary cause is neither disease nor declining demand for live donkeys, but instead a burgeoning market for their pelts.

Since ancient times the Chinese have consumed *ejiao*, a gelatin made by boiling and refining donkey skin to produce a tonic taken as an elixir. As the country grew richer in the 1990s and 2000s, demand for the product grew and fewer donkeys were needed for agriculture and transport. As a result, the number of donkeys in China fell from 11m in 1990 to 5m in 2016. Because donkeys are relatively poor breeders, China no longer has enough of them to satisfy its thirst for *ejiao*. One solution is to fake the product using the skin of other animals, such as pigs. But some manufacturers have now instituted DNA testing to ensure their *ejiao* is genuine. The other option is to import from abroad.

China's biggest sources are African. In Kenya, the price of a donkey soared by 325% during a six-month period in 2017. From

---

Hide and seek
Donkey population, % change 2011–16, selected countries

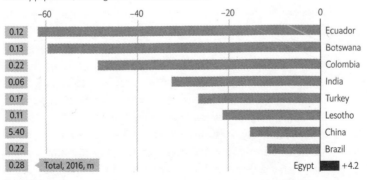

Source: FAO

Global assets

Donkey population, 2016

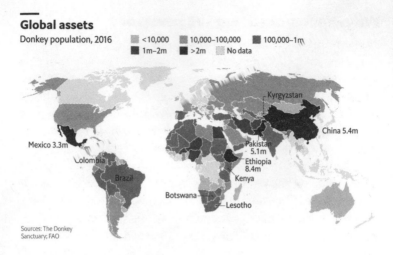

Sources: The Donkey
Sanctuary; FAO

2011 to 2016, the number of donkeys fell by 60% in Botswana and a fifth in Lesotho. But countries all over the world are getting in on the act. In Kyrgyzstan, which borders China, and in India, the donkey populations fell by a fifth during 2015 and 2016 alone. Farther afield, Colombia lost almost a tenth of its donkeys and Brazil around 5% over the same period. Some South American donkeys are transported more than 1,000km (620 miles) for slaughter, demonstrating the reach of the Chinese demand.

Poor farmers can hardly be blamed for selling their donkeys for sums that dwarf their value as draft animals. But in many cases the vendors are not the actual owners. Instead, thieves have begun stealing donkeys to take advantage of the surging prices, leaving farmers without their most prized labourers. In response, around 15 countries have taken measures to curb the donkey trade, for example by refusing permits for exports. In 2015 Pakistan became the first country to ban the export of donkey hides. Several African countries, including Botswana, now prohibit exports to China. The Donkey Sanctuary, a charity, wants an immediate halt to the trade. But with *ejiao* popular among China's middle classes, its government isn't listening. In January 2018 it boosted the industry by reducing the tariff on imports of donkey skins from 5% to 2%.

Why Japan has so much plutonium

Ten years after the incineration of Hiroshima and Nagasaki by American nuclear bombs, Japan embraced "atoms for peace", a policy of civilian nuclear power championed by Dwight Eisenhower, America's president. The dowry in this unlikely cold-war marriage of convenience was 6kg of enriched uranium, which Japan used to seed a nuclear-energy programme that would eventually provide it with about a third of its electricity. In 1988 Japan was permitted – under tight international controls – to enrich uranium and extract plutonium, employing the same technology used to make nuclear bombs. In 2018 the two governments extended the 1988 agreement. Japan has now amassed 47 tonnes of plutonium, enough to make 6,000 bombs. What is Japan doing with so much plutonium?

Plutonium is at the heart of Japan's tarnished dream of energy independence. Spent fuel from nuclear reactors can be reprocessed to extract plutonium, which is then recycled into mixed oxide (MOX) fuel. This was intended for use in Japan's reactors, but most of its nuclear power plants have been offline since the 2011 Fukushima disaster. Tougher safety checks have failed to reassure the nuclear-phobic public that the reactors can be restarted. And Japan's nuclear-energy fleet is ageing. Taro Kono, Japan's foreign minister, has admitted that this situation is "extremely unstable".

Japan's status as a plutonium superpower is increasingly under scrutiny. The government says it has no intention of building a bomb. But China and other countries question how long it can be allowed to stockpile plutonium. Analysts worry about a competitive build-up of plutonium in Asia. Moreover, Japan's stock of the material, which is weapons-grade, is reprocessed and stored in France and Britain. It is moved across the world in heavily armed convoys. America says those shipments and the storage of plutonium at civilian sites present a potential threat to non-proliferation goals: they could be redirected to make weapons, or targeted by terrorists. It is nudging its ally to start reducing the hoard.

One solution might be to fire up the Rokkasho plant, the centrepiece of Japan's nuclear-recycling policy. Rokkasho, in Japan's snowy north, could reprocess eight tonnes of plutonium a year. But it is three times over budget and two decades late (it is now supposed to open in March 2022). Even if it works someday, most of the reactors supposed to use its MOX fuel are offline. America could tighten the screws or even terminate the 1988 pact (a clause allows it to do so) though the robust bilateral alliance makes that very unlikely. That means Japan must either find a way to bury its cache underground – a huge and costly feat of engineering – or pay countries such as Britain and France to store it overseas, perhaps permanently. The most likely scenario is a continuation of the status quo, unstable as it is.

Why there is a world shortage of vanilla

Vanilla is one of the world's most popular spices, and an important ingredient in products ranging from chocolate to perfume. But it is getting harder to find. Vanilla-rich foods like ice-cream have been removed from shelves or become pricier. Chefs are making what they have go further. The wholesale price of vanilla has reached $500–600 per kilogram, when just a few years ago it fetched a tenth of that. What is happening?

Madagascar supplies 80–85% of the world's natural vanilla. In the 19th century the French introduced Bourbon vanilla, a tropical vine orchid native to Mexico and parts of South America, to their African island colony. Vanilla represents 20% of Madagascan exports, worth around $600m at current prices. But it is a difficult crop to grow. A vine takes three to four years to mature, or two years if grown from a large, good-quality cutting. The flowers open for just one day a year, so pollination is done by hand. Nine months later the green beans must be hand-picked when perfectly ripe to optimise their vanillin content (the compound that gives vanilla its flavour). Harvest lasts from May in northern Madagascar to August in the middle of the country, after the rainy season has brought the usual cyclones. Months of blanching, sweating and gradual drying in the sun are then necessary to produce the aromatic spice. Six hundred hand-pollinated blossoms yield about 6kg of green beans, which convert to 1kg of dried beans.

The price of Madagascar's vanilla was once set by the government, which formed a sort of vanilla cartel with nearby Comoros and Réunion. But such were the prices it demanded for vanilla that in the 1980s buyers turned their attention to the cheaper, poorer-quality version available elsewhere – in particular, from Indonesia. Madagascar's government was eventually forced to end its price-fixing regime. Exacerbating the pressure, food giants such as Unilever, Mondelez International and Nestlé also increased their use of synthetic vanillin, which can be produced from reliable sources such as wood pulp and petroleum. As a result, for 20 years

Madagascar's vanilla farmers earned a mere pittance, and many ended up leaving the business. But even with fewer producers the price of natural vanilla stayed low, suppressed by the availability of synthetic vanillin. It was not until public tastes started shifting towards all things natural that farmers' fortunes revived. From around 2011 some manufacturers began focusing once more on natural vanilla (while also changing their recipes to achieve the synthetic tastes with which consumers had grown familiar). In 2015 Nestlé announced plans to use only natural ingredients within five years, and rivals like Hershey followed suit. Demand has therefore surged, and with it prices – in part because vanilla vines take years to mature, and natural supplies are insufficient. Extreme weather, weak crop-security, and exporters who hoard inventory and speculate on further rises have also kept prices high.

This rise has not been without its challenges. To prevent theft of their now rather valuable crops, farmers have taken to harvesting the beans early, before they are mature, thereby reducing the overall quality of the crop. At the same time, the government needs to make greater efforts to enforce penalties for anyone caught dealing in unripe beans before the regional calendars allow. That would persuade farmers to leave beans on the vine until they are mature, improving both quality and yield. If it manages this, Madagascar could yet savour the benefits of its near-monopoly.

The battle for Colombia's sunken treasure

In May 1708 the *San José*, a 62-gun Spanish galleon, set sail from Portobelo, in what is now Panama, bound for Cartagena in Colombia. The ship carried 600 crew and a large fortune – 200 tonnes of gold, silver and emeralds belonging to the viceroy of Peru. She never reached her destination: in June that year she was sunk by a squadron of British ships. For more than three centuries her final resting place remained a mystery. But on December 4th 2015 Juan Manuel Santos, Colombia's president, announced that a team of archaeologists had found the wreck 30 miles off the Colombian coast. He promised to recover the ship and its contents, worth as much as $17bn, and build a museum in Cartagena to house them. Yet the galleon remains on the seabed. What explains the delay?

There is little agreement over who owns the *San José*. After five months of exploration the ship was located on November 27th 2015 by a team including the Colombian navy; Maritime Archaeology Consultants (MAC), a British firm; and the Woods Hole Oceanographic Institution, which provided an unmanned submarine. Colombia's government says the Submerged Cultural Heritage Law, passed in 2013, dictates that the wreck and its treasure belong to the state. Others dispute that. Spain's government says UNESCO's convention on underwater cultural heritage gives it rights to the ship. Sea Search Armada, an American exploration firm, claims it discovered the *San José* in 1981 and gave its location to the Colombian government. It believes it is due half the ship's treasure. The government says the galleon was found in a different spot, although the exact co-ordinates are a state secret.

With the wind in his sails, Mr Santos was eager to excavate and recover the ship. But the process has proved frustratingly slow. The project is estimated to cost $60m; Mr Santos wanted a public–private partnership agreement in which a company finances the ship's excavation and builds a laboratory and museum to preserve and display its treasures. In return, the company would receive up to 40% of any treasure not considered part of Colombia's cultural heritage, such as gold and silver ingots. In March 2018 the contract for the partnership was put out to public tender. The deadline for submissions was extended numerous times amid accusations of impropriety. Campaigners say the government unfairly favours MAC over other firms, a charge it denies.

Many Colombians bristle at the idea of sharing the ship's riches. In July 2018 a group of self-described "concerned citizens" sent a petition to a court in Bogotá to halt the public tender, arguing that it threatened Colombians' rights. The process was briefly suspended while the case was heard and then rejected. But there is a further twist: Mr Santos left office in August 2018. His successor, Iván Duque Márquez, must decide whether to go with the flow or change tack. Given their colonial past, Colombians are understandably wary of foreign profiteers. But with the wrecks of more than a thousand galleons and merchant ships thought to lie along the country's coastline, offering incentives to treasure-hunters seems a canny investment.

What is Brent crude, exactly?

Brent crude is the benchmark against which the majority of the 100m barrels of crude oil traded every day are priced. In October 2018 the price of Brent crude rose above $85 a barrel, its highest level in four years. But the black stuff that makes up the Brent benchmark comprises a tiny fraction of the world's extracted oil. So why is it used to determine the value of 60% of oil on international markets?

The international oil trade is relatively new. It was not until 1861 that the first deal between two countries was recorded, when the *Elizabeth Watts*, a cargo ship, took a consignment of oil from Pennsylvania to London. Before the second world war, oil was mainly traded regionally. After the war the market became increasingly global as the number of producers expanded. Its price was largely set by oil companies, and later by the 15 countries that make up OPEC, the oil-producers' cartel. It is only since the late 1980s that prices have been determined by international markets. As crude oil differs in quality and availability depending on where it comes from, producers and traders need a reliable benchmark against which to judge the correct price.

The most widely used benchmark is the price of Brent crude, oil extracted in the North Sea. Brent makes such a good benchmark because it is easy to refine into products such as petrol, so demand is consistent. Because it comes from the sea, output can be raised as required and extra oil tankers can be chartered to ship the stuff. Supply of the more easily refined but landlocked West Texas Intermediate (WTI) crude, a benchmark commonly used in America, is constrained by pipeline capacity. When the Brent benchmark was first adopted for widespread use in 1985, the oil came from Shell's Brent oilfield. But as production diminished, crude oil from other fields in the North Sea was added into the blend that makes up the benchmark. Today, the price of a barrel of Brent crude is taken from the most competitive of five different types of crude, only one of which actually comes from the Brent field. This has maintained the security and volume of supply essential for a reliable benchmark.

Although Brent crude is well established in the world's markets, its continued importance is not assured. North Sea oil reserves are being depleted. New sources of crude from outside the North Sea could help guard against supply-side price swings, but also affect Brent's consistent quality. WTI, the second-most-common benchmark, has been gaining influence after the American government lifted a ban on oil exports in 2015. In 2018 China launched Shanghai crude futures, an attempt to create an Asian benchmark to rival the two Western incumbents. Many of the trades pegged to this benchmark use the yuan, which could make China's currency more important in the global economy. Shanghai crude has had some success, but it needs to attract more foreign interest to become a global alternative. So Brent crude is still the most prevalent gauge of the price of oil, though competition could one day have it over a barrel.

Why China rents out its pandas

Pandas are cute, popular and expensive. So expensive, in fact, that the Malaysian government has reportedly considered handing its two adult pandas back to China, the country from which all pandas originate. As part of an agreement made in 2014 by its then prime minister, Najib Razak, Malaysia must pay China $1m each year to rent the bears until 2024. When a new Malaysian government took power in May 2018 it reviewed the deal, and in January 2019 its leader, Mahathir Mohamad, had to deny ministerial claims that the pandas would be returned early. Why does Malaysia have to pay so much?

China has offered pandas as gifts since the 7th century, when Empress Wu sent two bears to Japan. The tradition resurfaced under Mao Zedong. Russia and North Korea were given pandas during the cold war, and America received a pair after President Nixon's China trip in 1972. By giving its national animal to a foreign power, China can emphasise the closeness of political ties. But as China has grown increasingly capitalist, pandas have become an economic tool as well. Instead of giving them away, in the 1980s China started loaning them for $50,000 per month, with the bears and any offspring remaining Chinese property. But the bears were not offered to just any country. Kathleen Buckingham and Paul Jepson of Oxford University found recent panda loans coincided with trade deals that China had signed in Scotland, Canada and France. They argue that pandas form a key part of what the Chinese call *guanxi* – reciprocal relationships that can establish deeper and more trusting bonds between countries.

The animals' diplomatic importance has led to some controversy. In 2010 a pair of American-born panda cubs were returned to China just two days after China had expressed anger at Barack Obama's meeting with the Dalai Lama. The National Zoo in Washington, DC had asked for an extension of the loan deal for one cub, but China refused, and both cubs were sent back. The timing was interpreted by some as an act of punishment. Panda-related disputes have also clouded China's relationship with Taiwan: China's offer of two bears in 2005 was declined by Taiwan's then pro-independence government, which objected to their names (a play on the Chinese word for "united"). A later, more China-friendly government accepted the bears as part of a strategy of strengthening ties across the Taiwan Strait.

Some take issue with the very idea of loaning pandas. When two pandas were brought to Edinburgh Zoo in Scotland a few years ago, Ross Minett, the campaign director of a local animal-welfare charity, said the bears were "being exploited as diplomatic pawns in a commercial deal". The zoo itself did not mind: its visitor numbers increased by 4m in the two years after the bears' arrival. Thanks in part to pressure from WWF, a campaign group, China is meant to spend the rents from pandas on conservation. Whether it actually does so is unclear, but the number of research and conservation bases has quadrupled in the past 40 years. Increasing the size of the wild panda population is proving a rather tougher task, however. There were 1,100 bears in 1976; since then, that number has increased to just 1,864.

What a controversial pastry says about China's economy

Mooncakes are among the most divisive treats. For some the chewy pastries are delicacies on which to gorge during the Mid-Autumn Festival, a Chinese holiday. For others they are dry, dense and full of calories. But for economists they are something else entirely: an indicator of important trends in consumption, innovation, corruption and grey-market trading. Mooncakes play this role because of their status as gifts. Ahead of the mid-autumn holiday, companies give them to employees; business associates exchange them. Consumption of mooncakes is thus less a reflection of whether people enjoy the pastries (which are likened by some to edible hockey pucks), and more a measure of the health of the economy. So it was heartening to know that, amid rising trade tensions with America, the Chinese bakery association forecast that sales of mooncakes would rise by a solid 5–10% in September 2018.

Some observers fretted that Chinese consumers, burdened by rising debt, might start opting for cheaper goods. But consumers still plump for more expensive varieties of mooncakes rather than the classic nut-and-egg-yolk fillings. Shangri-La, a five-star hotel chain, won fans with its blueberry-cheese mooncake (dismissed by traditionalists as cheesecake). Judging by long queues at Häagen-Dazs stores, mooncake-shaped ice-cream sandwiches were also popular. At least 30 listed food companies – more than ever before – vied for a bite of the $2bn mooncake market in 2018.

Mooncakes have long given off a whiff of corruption. Businesses seeking favours from officials send lavishly wrapped boxes of them. When Xi Jinping, China's powerful president, intensified his anti-graft campaign in 2013, the mooncake market shrank by more than 20%. A rebound in 2015–18 naturally fuelled talk of a rebound in bribery, too. The government denied this. Yet the front page of the newspaper published by the Communist Party's anti-graft agency warned in September 2018 that although mooncakes are small, they could point to much bigger problems.

Perhaps the tastiest part of the consumption of mooncakes is what they reveal about China's grey economy. Scalpers hawking mooncake gift coupons took to Shanghai's streets in September 2018, as they do every year, standing outside busy subway stations and popular bakeries. Most economic studies describe scalping as a phenomenon that arises when scarce tickets to sporting events or concerts are resold at a hefty mark-up. Yet there is no shortage of mooncakes in China. Instead the problem is inefficient allocation: too many coupons are given to people who do not like them, so they decide to resell them. It is a reminder that although China's economy has plenty of inefficiencies, whether in the form of state-owned companies or gift-giving customs, it is also efficient enough to devise solutions.

Why Westerners are eating so much more chicken

Walk into any upscale supermarket in a big Western city and you will find a vegan section. This might lead you to believe that the number of people who will only eat plant-based foods is increasing. Perhaps it is, but surveys show that less than 10% of Europeans have cut meat entirely from their diets. According to Gallup, a polling firm, just 5% of American adults are vegetarians, a proportion that is virtually unaltered since 1999. But even though Westerners remain wary of ingesting tofu sausages, and are eating the same amounts of beef and pork, their diets have still changed significantly in recent decades. Data from the OECD, a club of mostly rich countries, show that since 1990 consumption of chicken per person has risen by 70% in rich countries.

What explains the growing importance of chicken in Western cuisine? One reason relates to health. In the 1980s doctors warned that eating too much saturated fat, which is found in red meat, could increase the risk of heart disease. And now, though doctors worry less about saturated fat, new evidence suggests that eating red meat can lead to colon cancer. In contrast, chicken's reputation as a relatively healthy meat has remained unscathed.

A second reason people are eating more chicken is that it has become cheaper. Poultry producers have been much more successful than producers of other meats at cutting costs. In 1960 a pound of chicken cost half as much as a pound of beef. This ratio has now fallen to one-third. Since the 1940s farmers have competed to produce bigger birds, which provide more meat. The use of antibiotics in industrial agriculture has allowed farmers to keep chickens in denser and dirtier conditions than ever before. A study by Martin Zuidhof from the University of Alberta found that the average broiler chicken, raised for meat, weighed 4.2kg at 56 days of age in 2005, up from just 0.9kg in 1957. Bigger chickens, living closer together, become more efficient at converting grain into meat as they lack the space to move around (though the use of antibiotics in chicken farming is now declining).

These two factors have created a boon for consumers eager to scoff large amounts of lean protein. But they may want to listen to animal-welfare advocates. Nearly all of the chickens' weight gain comes in the form of muscle mass, which means that their organs have to work harder than before. Cardiovascular problems are common, as is lameness. Broiler chickens are now so big that their muscles prevent them from getting on top of each other to mate. Consequently, the growth of birds chosen to be breeders must be stunted through calorie restriction while they are young. Modern chickens may be a source of healthy meals for humans, but their own well-being has been compromised even further to provide it.

The global rise in houseplants

People born after 1980 have been slower than previous generations to settle down. Some want to explore the world before they get married and have kids. Others simply cannot afford to buy a house. But they can afford houseplants – and many are finding that nurturing them is a more manageable form of domesticity.

Since the turn of the century, exports of plants from the Netherlands – by far the world's biggest producer of plant life – have increased by 50%, from $6bn in 2000 to $9bn in 2016. In that year Europeans spent some €36bn ($42bn) on houseplants and flowers. And in America, millennials are thought to account for fully one-third of houseplant sales. Amazon, the world's biggest online retailer, began selling plants last year, and direct-to-consumer start-ups such as Patch and The Sill have cropped up, delivering leafy goods in pretty pots to doorsteps everywhere.

Interest in houseplants as measured by internet-search data has closely tracked the surge in sales. The number of Google searches for succulents has risen tenfold since 2010, and other green plants

Growing interest
Worldwide Google searches for selected house plants, 100=peak

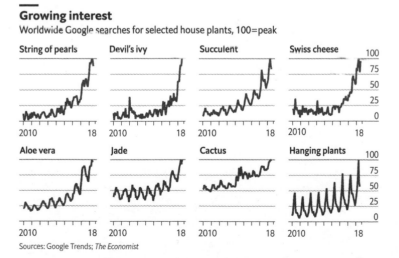

Sources: Google Trends; *The Economist*

have had similar spurts of popularity. The data are highly seasonal: interest blossoms in the spring but is relatively dormant by December.

What explains the growth in greenery? Young people are more likely than their elders to live in urban flats without gardens. Although houseplants grow and require care, they are neither as demanding nor as costly as pets or children. Instagram, a photo-sharing platform, can also be credited for causing a spike in interest in cacti and other plants: #plantsofinstagram boasts more than 3m photographs – double that of a previous millennial fad, #avocadotoast.

Why it matters if the Caspian is a sea or a lake

What is the Caspian? For 20 years Azerbaijan, Iran, Kazakhstan, Russia and Turkmenistan, which surround it, have disagreed over whether this body of water is a lake or a sea. Like many lakes, it does not feed into an ocean, but it is sea-like in its size and depth. The distinction is not merely semantic, but has economic, military and political implications. That is because lakes' surfaces and beds are divided up equally by bordering countries, whereas seas are governed by the UN's Law of the Sea. The surface and bed are allotted, nearer to shore, according to the length of relevant coastline. When Iran and the Soviet Union were the only two countries to border the Caspian, a series of bilateral treaties identified it as a lake that they divided equally. Iran, which has a short Caspian coast, still prefers this idea. Kazakhstan, which has the longest shore on the Caspian, is among the countries that prefer to call it a sea.

The Caspian basin and surrounding area are rich in hydro-carbons, including 48bn barrels of oil and over 8trn cubic metres of gas, according to the US Energy Information Administration. The surrounding countries already exploit the reserves close to their coasts, where jurisdiction is the same regardless of whether the Caspian is a lake or a sea. But many hydrocarbon deposits in the south of the Caspian are disputed by Azerbaijan, Iran and Turkmenistan. In addition, Turkmenistan, with the world's fourth-largest gas reserves, hopes to construct a trans-Caspian pipeline to export gas to Europe. Russia has long opposed the pipeline. It cites environmental concerns, but may be rather more motivated by a desire to maintain its market dominance.

On August 12th 2018 the leaders of the five Caspian countries met in the Kazakh city of Aqtau to determine the water's status. The resulting Convention on the Legal Status of the Caspian Sea was a compromise. Despite its name, it determines that the Caspian is neither lake nor sea. The surface is to be treated as a sea, with states granted jurisdiction over 15 nautical miles of water from their coasts and fishing rights over an additional ten miles. But the seabed and its lucrative mineral deposits are not allocated in precise form. This division of the spoils is left to countries to agree on a bilateral basis. The convention also permits the construction of pipelines, which only require the approval of the countries whose seabed they cross, subject to environmental provisions, and forbids non-Caspian countries from deploying military vessels in the water.

The convention most clearly benefits Russia in the short term. Russia secures the dominance of its Caspian sea fleet, from which it has launched missiles at targets in Syria. The convention also serves as a show of Russo-Iranian co-operation in the face of American sanctions, and lets Russia reassert its ties to Caspian states in the context of rising Chinese influence in the region. The convention's benefits for the other Caspian states are more ambiguous. Kazakhstan will benefit from a firmer framework for the jurisdiction of its offshore Kashagan oilfield, but that is already in operation. The feasibility of trans-Caspian pipelines, taking oil from Kazakhstan and gas from Turkmenistan to Azerbaijan, was reaffirmed, though these were technically already permissible under international law. It is unclear if the other Caspian states are still able to prevent their construction by citing environmental concerns. But a resolution of the disputed area in the southern Caspian remains elusive. Iran's president, Hassan Rouhani, made clear that more agreements will be required to divide the seabed into territorial zones. The Caspian's surface may be closer to a sea, but the fate of the subsoil remains a work in progress.

Sexual selection: love, sex and marriage

Why civil partnerships are becoming more popular, even among straight couples

On June 27th 2018 Rebecca Steinfeld and Charles Keidan emerged triumphant from the British Supreme Court. The judges had ruled that it was discriminatory for British law to deny a heterosexual couple such as them the right to a civil partnership, when same-sex couples have that right. But while Ms Steinfeld and Mr Keidan celebrated, many heterosexual couples in Britain may have wondered what they were missing out on.

Civil partnerships first appeared in Europe in the late 1980s and 1990s, as a compromise between supporters and opponents of gay marriage. They offered gay couples a legal partnership with most of the rights of marriage, without actually granting them the right to marry. Many gay-rights activists saw this as an unsatisfactory fudge, creating a system that was inherently inferior to marriage, and continued to push for the real thing. In the 2000s, with public opinion in many Western countries continuing to soften, their efforts bore fruit: today, 27 countries allow same-sex marriage. As they legalised gay marriage, countries that had previously had civil-partnership laws dealt with them in different ways. Some, like Ireland and Sweden, abolished civil partnerships altogether; they saw no need to keep a much-maligned compromise once everyone could get married.

But in seven European countries, and some states of America and Australia, civil partnerships are still permitted, even though gay marriage is also legal. In Britain and Finland, they are only available to same-sex couples, whereas in France and the Netherlands, they are available to heterosexual couples too. The rights enshrined in these partnerships vary from place to place. The British versions are marriage in all but name, as are Dutch "registered partnerships". In France, though, a civil solidarity pact (PACS) confers only some of the tax benefits and adoption rights of marriage, and can also be annulled far more easily. Remarkably, civil partnerships in some countries have become increasingly popular among heterosexual couples. From 2012 to 2016, the number of heterosexual couples in France choosing to enter into a PACS increased by 20% to 184,000, while the number of marriages fell by 8% to 225,000.

This enthusiasm for civil partnerships might perplex gay-marriage advocates, who for a long time regarded them as inadequate. But there are many reasons why a couple might prefer a civil partnership. In places like France, they allow couples to opt for a looser form of commitment either permanently or for a trial period before choosing to marry. Others might prefer civil partnerships for personal or ideological reasons, even when they confer the same rights as marriage. Equal Civil Partnerships, a British advocacy group, suggests that some people "want to avoid the social expectations, pressures and traditions surrounding marriage" in favour of "a more modern form of legal union". Ms Steinfeld and Mr Keidan took the government to court over civil partnerships because they viewed marriage as sexist and patriarchal: they told reporters that they associated it with a legacy of treating women as property. The ruling in their favour did not change Britain's civil partnership law, but in October 2018 the government said it would extend the right to enter a civil partnership to everyone.

Why expensive weddings are a bad idea

Getting hitched is not cheap. Various estimates put the cost of a typical British wedding at anywhere between £18,000 and £25,000 ($23,000 and $32,000), or roughly eight to eleven months of disposable income for the median household. That would pay for less than half the luxury toilets at the royal wedding that took place between Prince Harry, the sixth in line to the throne, and Meghan Markle, an American actress, according to guesses made by bridebook.co.uk, a wedding-planning website.

Yet a flashy wedding might simply be a recipe for a flustered couple. A global survey in 2017 of 16,000 brides and grooms by

---

For richer, for poorer
Global wedding survey, 2017

By wedding cost, $'000 ▨ 1–10 ▨ 11–30 ▨ 31–95 ▨ 96–500 ▨ 500+

Couples saying this priority is "very important", %

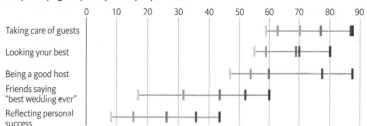

Couples who contributed to cost of own wedding, %

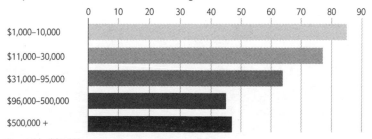

Source: Splendid Insights

Splendid Insights, a market-research firm, found that those who spent more than $500,000 on their big day were much more preoccupied with showing off to their guests than those on a tight budget. They were nearly five times more likely to say that "reflecting a certain level of success" was "very important" than those who spent less than $10,000. They were also more reliant on financial assistance from others to do so. Fewer than half of respondents in the top-spending bracket had contributed to the costs of their wedding, compared with five-sixths of those at the bottom.

Nor is a luxurious nuptial a guarantee of everlasting bliss. A study published in 2015 by two economists at Emory University found that among couples of the same income, education and race, those who had married on a higher budget were more likely to get divorced. They were also more stressed about paying off their wedding debts, despite any extra help they might have received from family. Such money worries may not have troubled Harry and Meghan. But it might discourage others from dreaming about a wedding in a castle.

How India decriminalised homosexuality

Campaigners for gay rights have enjoyed a sequence of victories in the West. The battleground has often been gay marriage, which is now recognised in nearly 30 countries. But in India, the world's largest democracy, the situation has been very different. Homosexuality itself was regarded as a crime there, albeit one that was rarely prosecuted. Untold millions of Indians were designated as felons by a series of judicial rulings issued as recently as 2013. Then on September 6th 2018, being gay was decriminalised. What happened?

Section 377 of the Indian Penal Code was to blame for the predicament. A holdover from colonial times, the 19th-century law forbade "carnal intercourse against the order of nature with any man, woman or animal". That language could be, and still is, read to prohibit bestiality and incest. But it was also held to refer to gay sex, as well as oral and anal sex practised by heterosexual couples. The threat of punishment was held over the head of every gay person living in India, by anyone who might wish to harass or extort them, and used to drive their civic organisations underground. Section 377 was not challenged in the courts until the 1990s. It idled in the judicial doldrums until matters took a hopeful turn in 2009, when the Delhi High Court ruled that it could not be used to ban consensual relations between adults without being unconstitutionally discriminatory. But in 2013 that hope was quashed by a Supreme Court ruling that stood out for its shoddy writing and reasoning. Proceeding from the supposition that people engaging in the proscribed sex acts were members of a "miniscule [sic] minority" – the correct spelling is "minuscule" – the highest court upheld the ban on the grounds that only the legislature had the right to say whether they could be treated as a criminal class. In India's parliament, alas, there was only the thinnest of support for gay rights.

So the path to decriminalisation led back through the courts. In legal terms the way was simple enough. The language of Section

377 had to be reinterpreted such that "the order of nature" could admit a greater variety of sex. The rest of 377 could be, and was, left to stand. First the case had to be referred to a larger bench of the Supreme Court than the one that issued the ruling in 2013, in light of relatively liberal judgments reached since then, such as those recognising the rights of transgender Indians, and a general right to privacy. Then there was the matter of gathering a bunch of eloquent plaintiffs. That seems to have gone most of the way towards demonstrating to five of the Supreme Court's senior justices that sexual orientation was an unfair basis on which to discriminate among citizens. All that was left was for the judges to take turns extolling the principle of justice for all and lamenting the injustice that had been done to gay Indians for so many years.

The judges' statements were largely unopposed in the political realm. The conservative government of Narendra Modi had withdrawn its stand against the reinterpretation in July 2018. Nearly everyone writing about the case started by mentioning the penal code's British origin, a sure way to unite right and left in a post-colonial society. Some members of the Supreme Court may have wished to burnish their liberal credentials, before turning to more contentious matters like the government's brief to expand its troubled universal-identification system, or to allow a Hindu group to build a temple on the site of a razed mosque. Regardless of the larger context in India, and however symbolic the gesture, there was much to celebrate in the outcome. Popular attitudes towards sexual minorities have changed rapidly in the West. As recently as 2004, an American presidential campaign could be successfully run on opposition to gay marriage. Legal victories led the way there, and may yet hasten fuller expressions of equality in India as well.

How gender stereotypes are built into Mandarin

Gender bias in language is exercising Europe's linguists. A French grammar book published in 2017 ignited debates about an old grammatical rule that holds that masculine forms of words trump the feminine. In similar vein, Spanish politicians have proposed editing the constitution to include a reference to female workers ("workers" in the masculine, and therefore universal, form are already mentioned). And German grammarians have been mulling an update to dictionaries to include new, genderless versions of words. In China, however, the debate is rather quieter. Yet Mandarin – spoken by 70% of Chinese people – has gender bias, too. It shares some issues with other languages: female bosses, for example, are typically identified as such (eg, woman-boss), whereas male ones are not. But unlike some European tongues, Mandarin does not assign genders to nouns. It has a different, and inaudible, problem: some of its written characters ascribe negative stereotypes to women.

Chinese characters are made up of smaller components, called radicals, that come in two forms. Phonetic radicals give clues about a character's pronunciation; semantic ones give clues about its meaning. For example, the radical for "speech" is semantic and is found on the left side of characters associated with speech, such as: "language", "words", "to request", "to chat", "to thank" and so on. Chinese dictionaries are often sorted by radical, so these characters are listed together. Similarly, the Chinese radical for "woman" is found in the characters for "mother", "sister" and "aunt".

But the "woman" radical is also found in the characters and words for "jealousy", "suspicion", "slave", "devil" and "rape". It appears in some more positive instances, such as "good" and "safety", but even these characters rely on stereotypes: "good" depicts a woman next to a child, and "safety" is represented by a woman under a roof. The woman radical itself is thought to derive from an image of a woman bending over with her hands clasped together. The word for man, by contrast, is made up of radicals meaning "field" and "power". Chinese grammar, especially word order, can also be said to favour men. The word for "parents" is "father and mother", in that order; "children" is sometimes depicted as "son and daughter". Most ironically, as one linguist has noted, the phrase for "gender equality" puts the male character before the female one.

But progress is possible. In 2015 curators used the traditional character for illicit sexual relations – three women radicals, one on top of two others, to suggest multiple affairs by a man – as the name of an exhibit on violence against women. A year later a group of female typographers published a book of characters that they had made up. One put the radicals for "walking" and "woman" together to convey the idea that women's roles can be outside the home. Inventing new characters is rather easier than abolishing existing ones, though. China's written language is a source of national pride, persisting despite the difficulty it imposes. But it means that anyone who spends hours learning Chinese characters will also learn the stereotypes built into them.

How a typical American birth costs as much as delivering a royal baby

A royal birth is always heralded with great fanfare, and the arrival of the Duchess of Cambridge's third baby on April 23rd 2018 was no exception. Throngs of reporters waited for updates outside the Lindo Wing, a luxurious private maternity ward in London that has often been used by British royals and that boasts a comprehensive wine list for celebrating parents.

Yet the price of delivering the new prince, who is fifth in line to the British throne, was probably slightly less than that of an average American baby. In 2015, the Lindo Wing charged £5,670 ($8,900) for 24 hours in a deluxe room and a non-Caesarean delivery. A survey in the same year by the International Federation of Health Plans found that the average fee for such a delivery in the United States was $10,808. That rises to roughly $30,000 after accounting for care given before and after a pregnancy, according to Truven Health Analytics, a company providing health-care data. Insurers cover

A princely sum
Average price of normal birth delivery, in private sector, 2015 or latest, $'000

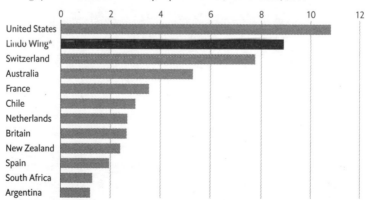

Sources: International Federation of
Health Plans; St Mary's Hospital   *Deluxe room package, St Mary's Hospital, London

most of the cost, but parents are still left with an average bill of about $3,000. In many European countries, free maternity care is available.

The irresistible rise of internet dating

For most of human history, the choice of life partner was limited by class, location and parental diktat. In the 19th and 20th centuries those constraints were weakened, at least in the West. The bicycle increased young people's choices immeasurably; so did city life. But freed from their villages, people faced new difficulties: how to work out who was interested, who was not and who might be, if only they knew you were.

In 1995, less than a year after Netscape launched the first widely used web browser, a site called match.com was offering to help people answer those questions. As befits a technology developed in the San Francisco Bay area, online dating first took off among gay men and geeks. But it soon spread, proving particularly helpful for people needing a way back into the world of dating after the break-up of a long-term relationship.

By 2010, nearly 70% of same-sex relationships were starting

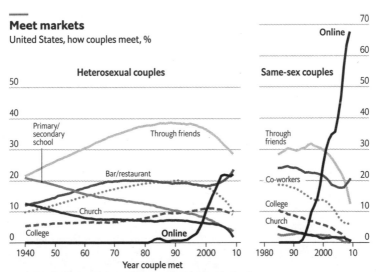

Meet markets

United States, how couples meet, %

Source: "Searching for a mate: the rise of the internet as a social intermediary", M. J. Rosenfeld and R. J. Thomas, *American Sociological Review*, 2012

online, and the internet had overtaken churches, neighbourhoods, classrooms and offices as a setting in which Americans might meet a partner of the opposite sex. Couples who had met online became commonplace. Today dating sites and apps account for about a sixth of the first meetings that lead to marriage. Globally, at least 200m people use digital dating services every month. In America more than a third of marriages now start with an online match-up. The internet is the second-most-popular way for Americans to meet people of the opposite sex, and is fast catching up with real-world "friend of a friend" introductions.

Research has found that marriages in America between people who meet online are likely to last longer; such couples profess to be happier than those who met offline. Precious little evidence exists to show that opportunities online are encouraging infidelity. In America, divorce rates climbed until just before the advent of the internet, and have fallen since. And the fact that online daters have so much more choice can break down barriers: evidence suggests that the internet is boosting interracial marriages by bypassing homogenous social groups.

Does owning a car, or a TV, mean you have more sex?

"My car's out back if you're ready to take that long walk, from your front porch to my front seat: the door's open but the ride ain't free." Anyone acquainted with the songs of Bruce Springsteen will be familiar with the idea that driving around a lot is associated with an active sex life. A paper by Adrienne Lucas and Nicholas Wilson, economists at the University of Delaware and Reed College respectively, provides empirical evidence for such a link.

Using household-fertility surveys of 3.2m women and 640,000 men in 80 developing countries, they were able to examine which durable consumer goods were linked with a higher propensity to get it on. Because the data were collected over a wide geographical range between 1986 and 2016, the authors had to control for where and when the surveys had been conducted. They also accounted for age, education, population density, marital status, knowledge about sexual health and the total number of durable goods owned (as a proxy for wealth).

After holding all of those factors constant, the 9% of respondents who owned a car and the 15% who had a motorcycle stood out as an unusually lustful bunch. Men and women who drive motor vehicles were about 5% more likely to have got lucky in the preceding week than were people of the same demographic profile who lacked chrome wheels and fuel injectors. Why? Cars and motorcycles are expensive items, so the correlation between owning them and having sex could simply show that the wealthiest people also have the strongest libidos. However, refrigerators, televisions and "improved" floors (which means those made from something other than dirt) are not cheap either, and were generally linked with having less sex.

Although the sizes of the effects found in the study are quite small, its sample size is so large that the negative values for refrigerators and televisions among women and for improved floors among men are highly statistically significant, and therefore

Sex drive

Change in probability of having sex in preceding week, for owners of consumer goods, among 3.2m women and 640,000 men in 80 developing countries, 1986–2016, %

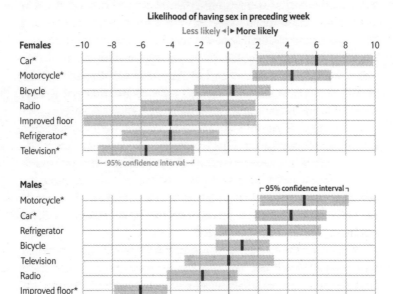

Source: "Does television kill your sex life?", A. Lucas and N. Wilson, National Bureau of Economic Research, 2018

*Statistically significant

unlikely to be a random quirk in the data. The same is true of the positive values among both sexes for purring engines. Ms Lucas suggests hypotheses that might account for each of these relationships. Vehicles could make it easier to find lovers on different edges of town, or to get home on time. Women who save up for fridges and men who save up for renovated floors might be better at delaying their gratification (or have their hands already full during leisure time). And television's chastening effect on women could be due to changing their attitudes about sex, as other studies in developing countries have suggested. Or perhaps they have merely found something more entertaining to do.

How young men are changing their definitions of sexual harassment

The final months of 2017 brought an unprecedented flood of allegations about sexual harassment in the workplace and beyond. Harvey Weinstein, a Hollywood movie mogul, was the first of many powerful men to be toppled by the #MeToo movement, as victims shared their experiences of sexual abuse. Celebrities, among them household names such as Louis C.K., a comedian, and Kevin Spacey, an actor, were forced – at least temporarily – from the stage.

Following the rise of #MeToo, have definitions of unacceptable behaviour towards women changed? In October 2017 *The Economist* commissioned YouGov, a pollster, to ask more than 6,800 people from four Western countries about their attitudes towards sexual harassment and misconduct. A year later YouGov repeated the poll to find out if those perceptions have shifted. Some had, but not in ways that you might expect.

Rather than behaving more respectfully around women, young men in particular seemed to have become more accepting of inappropriate behaviour. This was especially true in Britain and America. The share of men under 30 who thought that a stranger flashing his genitals at a woman constituted sexual harassment, for example, dropped from 97% to 79% in Britain, and from 91% to 78% in America. YouGov's data showed similar declines among young men when it came to requesting sexual favours and making sexual jokes. Overall the share of British men aged 18 to 29 who felt that these acts represented sexual harassment dropped by 14 percentage points in just one year.

Attitudes among other respondents were less mutable. Opinions among men aged 65 and above seemed barely to have shifted in Britain, France and Germany. And the two surveys showed little change in women's opinions on where to draw the line; overall, their opinions had shifted by less than two percentage points on average. #MeToo succeeded in attracting lots of attention. But there is an awfully long way to go before men – intentionally or not – stop overstepping boundaries.

Crying wolf

"Which of the following would you consider to be sexual harassment if a man, who was not a romantic or sexual partner or friend, did them to a woman?"
By age group* and sex, % responding "sexual harassment"†

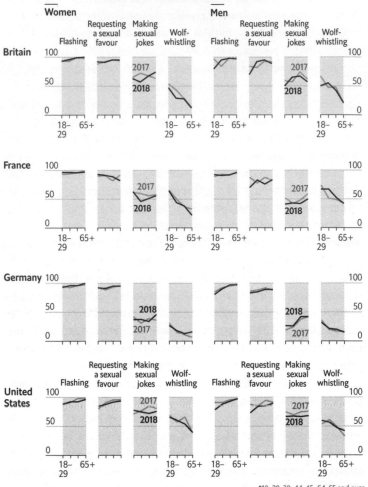

Sources: YouGov; *The Economist*

*18–29, 30–44, 45–64, 65 and over
†Surveyed Oct–Nov 2017 and Oct–Nov 2018

Why the number of abortions in America is at a historic low

Of all the controversies thrown up by America's cultural wars, abortion remains perhaps the most divisive. This was the issue that Ronald Reagan used to try to unite northern Catholics and southern evangelical Protestants behind his Republican presidential bid in 1980. When he succeeded, Democrats responded in kind by becoming the party of pro-choice crusaders. Over the years the battles between the pro-life and pro-choice camps have become more acrimonious, even violent, with death threats, firebombs and, in a few instances, the murder of doctors or other staff at clinics that perform abortions. But while the arguments have continued to rage, the number of abortions has actually dropped recently. According to figures recently released by the Centres for Disease Control and Prevention (CDC), in 2006 there were 842,855 abortions, a rate of 15.9 per 1,000 women, while in 2015 there were 638,169 abortions, a rate of 11.8 abortions per 1,000 women.

Abortions are now at their lowest level since the passage in 1973 of *Roe v Wade*, the Supreme Court's ruling that declared abortion a constitutional right. The drop can be seen in all age groups, but it is especially pronounced among teenagers. From 2006 to 2015, the abortion rate for 15- to 19-year-olds more than halved. The report also showed that abortions are being performed earlier in pregnancy, and therefore more safely. The percentage performed during the first six weeks of gestation rose by 11%.

The reasons for these changing numbers offer grounds for hope. As has happened across the developed world, the number of unintended pregnancies has fallen in America as the use of contraceptives has spread, particularly among young people. Yet there is also cause for concern. America differs from many rich countries in introducing restrictions on access to abortion that make it harder to get, less safe and much costlier. Between 2010 and 2016 32 states enacted 338 such restrictions. In September 2018 a three-judge panel on the Eighth Circuit Court of Appeals overturned a lower-court ruling that had blocked Missouri from enforcing regulations that could close all but one of the state's abortion clinics. In December 2018 Ohio's House of Representatives passed one of the country's most restrictive abortion bills, which would ban abortions in instances where a fetal heartbeat can be detected. (This can be as early as six weeks into a pregnancy, when most women are unaware they are pregnant.) The measure has no exceptions for rape or incest, only for a medical emergency or if an abortion would save a woman's life.

The CDC findings came at a worrying time for abortion-rights activists. In addition to the increasingly bold pushes from conservative lawmakers to all but ban abortions, they were fretting that Neil Gorsuch and Brett Kavanaugh, President Donald Trump's appointees to the Supreme Court, could help overturn *Roe v Wade*. This would allow state legislatures to introduce strict abortion laws without the risk that they would be branded unconstitutional. In four states (Louisiana, Mississippi, North Dakota and South Dakota) that have so-called trigger laws, abortions would immediately become illegal if *Roe v Wade* falls. This argument will not end soon.

The persistence of child marriages in Africa

Three out of four girls in Niger are married before they are 18, giving this poor west African country the world's highest rate of child marriage. The World Bank says it is one of only a very small number to have seen no reduction in recent years; the rate has even risen slightly. The country's minimum legal age of marriage for girls is 15, but some brides are as young as nine.

Across Africa child marriage stubbornly persists. Of the roughly 700m women living today who were married before they were 18, 125m are African. Among poor rural families the rate has not budged since 1990. The UN Children's Fund (UNICEF) estimates that, on current trends, almost half the world's child brides by 2050 will be African. But some countries have shown that they can keep young girls out of wedlock. In Ethiopia, once among Africa's top five

—
Cradle snatchers
Share of women married before 18, by age group
2017, %

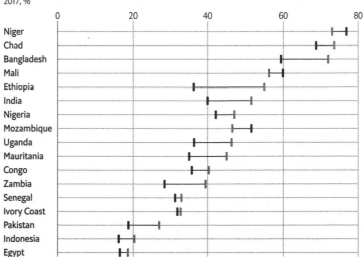

Sources: World Bank; International Centre for Research on Women

countries for child marriage, the practice has dropped by a third in the past decade – the world's sharpest decline, says the World Bank. The government wants to eradicate child marriage entirely by 2025.

Education is vital. "You generally don't find a child bride in school," notes a UNICEF expert in Ethiopia. Its government spends more on education as a proportion of its budget than other African countries. More than a third of Ethiopian girls enrol in secondary schools. In Niger the figure is less than a fifth.

Working assumptions: the world of employment

Why people are working longer

The golden years of retirement, when decades of toil are traded for some downtime, are starting later. In the mid-1980s, 25% of American men aged 65–69 worked; today, nearly 40% do. The situation is the same for younger men. In 1994, 53% of 60- to 64-year-olds worked; now 63% do. American women are working longer too, and similar upticks have been witnessed in Japan and parts of western Europe. Because unhealthy workers tend to retire earlier, many attribute the ageing workforce of today to improvements in health. Mortality rates for American men in their 60s have declined by 40% since 1980; for women, they have fallen by 30%. Education and occupation are also relevant. In the countries of the OECD, a club of mostly rich countries, the share of 55- to 64-year-olds with a college education has increased in the past three decades, and better-educated people, doing white-collar jobs, tend to work longer. In a similar vein, the fact that modern jobs in general are less physically taxing than those of yore allows all people to work for longer or look for jobs suitable to their advancing years.

But these are not in fact the primary drivers of the greying workforce, suggests Courtney Coile, an economist at Wellesley College. Social-security reforms and other institutional changes also play a central role. In recent decades, many countries and companies have altered the way they fund pensions. About half of Americans working in the private sector participate in employer-sponsored plans. In the 1980s a third were "defined benefit" (DB) schemes, under which a company pays its retired employees a predetermined lump sum depending on tenure, age and past earnings. Now, though, "defined contribution" (DC) plans, for which employees contribute a percentage of their paycheques to their retirement fund, have largely supplanted DB plans. These are generally lower than DB pensions (hence their popularity with employers), so their recipients cannot afford to retire so early. By working longer, they increase the size of the pot. Researchers reckon the growth in DC plans has led to a five-month increase in the median retirement age.

Reductions in the generosity of social security and disability insurance have also had an impact. Since the 1990s, Italy, Germany, Japan and others have raised the minimum age at which citizens can accept retirement benefits. The labour-force participation rates for older workers there have risen in lock-step, with a one- to two-year lag. A final factor is the increased number of women in the workforce: across 12 developed countries, about 44% more women hold a job now than in 1995. And, like men, they are working longer. Given that married couples often retire at the same time, this "co-ordination", which sees men working longer to keep up with hard-working wives, can have profound effects. In Canada, for example, it could explain around half the change in the labour-force participation rates of married men aged 55–64.

This is good news. The "lump of labour" fallacy holds that older workers threaten economic prosperity by holding onto jobs that would otherwise go to younger workers. (The same argument had been used to exclude women from the workforce.) In fact, the economies of many countries with ageing workforces are growing quite quickly. Older workers use their wages to buy goods and services made by other workers. And as Lisa Laun of Sweden's Institute for Evaluation of Labour Market and Education Policy points out, with more workers, of whatever age, tax revenues and pension contributions rise. That means a larger pie for everyone.

Why so few nurses are men

Ask health professionals in any country what the biggest problem in their health-care system is, and one of the most common answers is the shortage of nurses. In ageing rich countries demand for nursing care is becoming increasingly insatiable. Britain's National Health Service, for example, has 40,000-odd nurse vacancies. Poor countries struggle with the emigration of nurses for greener pastures. One obvious solution seems to be neglected: recruit more men. Typically, just 5–10% of nurses registered in a given country are men. Why so few?

Views of nursing as a "woman's job" have deep roots. Florence Nightingale, who established the principles of modern nursing in the 1860s, insisted that men's "hard and horny" hands were "not fitted to touch, bathe and dress wounded limbs". In Britain, the Royal College of Nursing, the profession's union, did not even admit men as members until 1960. Some nursing schools in America started admitting men only in 1982, after a Supreme Court ruling forced them to. Senior nurse titles such as "sister" (a ward manager) and "matron" (which in some countries is used for men as well) do not help matters. Unsurprisingly, some older people do not even know that men can be nurses too. Male nurses often encounter patients who assume they must be doctors.

Another problem is that beliefs about what a nursing job entails are often outdated – in ways that may be particularly off-putting for men. In films, nurses are commonly portrayed as the helpers of heroic male doctors. In fact, nurses do most of their work independently and are the first responders to patients in crisis. To dispel myths, nurse-recruitment campaigns now showcase nursing as a professional job with career progression, specialisms like anaesthetics, cardiology or emergency care, and the need for skills relating to technology, innovation and leadership. But attracting men without playing to gender stereotypes can be tricky. "Are you man enough to be a nurse?", the slogan of an American campaign, was understandably mired in controversy.

Nursing is not a career many boys aspire to, or are encouraged to consider. Only two-fifths of British parents say they would be proud if their son became a nurse. Because of all this, men who go into nursing are usually already closely familiar with the job. Some are following in the career footsteps of their mothers. Others decide that the job would suit them after they see a male nurse care for a relative, or they themselves receive care from a male nurse when in hospital. Although many gender stereotypes about jobs and caring have crumbled, nursing has, so far, remained impervious.

Are gender quotas good for business?

California is on its way to becoming the first American state to mandate gender diversity in companies at board level. A law passed in September 2018 requires publicly traded firms headquartered in California to have at least one woman on their board by the end of 2019. By 2021 they will be required to give women at least 40% of board seats. "It's not only the right thing to do. It's good for a company's bottom line." So said Hannah-Beth Jackson, one of the senators who proposed the bill. Some business leaders are unconvinced. Are they right to worry?

Norway pioneered this approach. From 2008 it obliged listed companies to have women in at least 40% of board seats or face dissolution. Over the following five years more than a dozen countries, mostly in western Europe, adopted similar quotas. In Belgium, France and Italy firms that fail to comply can be fined, dissolved or banned from paying directors. Germany, Spain and the Netherlands prefer quotas without sanctions. Britain opted for guidelines, and names and shames companies that fall short. In some countries, the share of women among directors of large companies has grown four- or five-fold since 2007.

Nearly two-thirds of public firms in California have fewer than two female directors. Opponents of quotas say that this reflects the scarcity of women in upper management. A quota, they warn, would see boards being stuffed with inexperienced, token women. Another concern is that a small number of highly qualified women, known as "golden skirts", would be stretched thinly across too many boards. But in Europe, such fears have not been realised. In large listed European companies, "golden trousers" are almost as common: 15% of male directors sit on three or more boards, while 19% of female directors do. Worries that quotas would lead to the appointment of under-qualified female directors also appear misplaced. A study of Italy's 33% quota found that female directors at the biggest firms were more likely than their pre-quota predecessors to have professional degrees and qualifications. Norway's quota led to a similar outcome. Elsewhere the picture has been more mixed, however, with female directors appointed after quotas likely to be younger, less experienced and, in some countries, foreign.

Does any of this affect how well companies do? Some "snapshot" studies show that companies with more women on their boards have better returns and are less likely to be beset by fraud or shareholder battles. But causation is hard to prove. Studies comparing firms' performance before and after quotas were introduced have been inconclusive. Some have found positive effects on firms' results; others the opposite. One Italian study found an initial increase in share price when female directors were elected to firms affected by the quota. But it found no effect on any of seven measures of firms' performance, including profit, output, debt and return on assets. A French study offers one clue for why the addition of more women has not made a consistent difference. It concluded that the country's new quota system led to changes in the way the boards made decisions, but there was no change in the substance of the decisions. It also found that the process did not change because the new members were women, but because they were likely to be outsiders. Perhaps it is too early to judge the effect of quotas on companies' performance. But if Europe's experience offers any guidance, expectations that California's new law could either dramatically boost or hurt corporate performance are exaggerated.

What men who make less than their wives say about their earnings

"Manning up" normally refers to stoicism in the face of hardship. But men who earn less than their wives tend to "man up" as well – by exaggerating their income when responding to survey-takers. That is the surprising conclusion of a paper published by researchers at America's Census Bureau. Their comparison between self-reported data and actual tax filings over the past ten years shows that, when outshone by their better halves, men overstate what they earn by 2.9%, while women report earning 1.5% less than they actually do.

The share of women who earn more than their husbands has risen steeply in America since the 1980s. In 1987, about 18% of women were the main breadwinners in households where both spouses worked. By 2010, that figure had jumped to almost 30%. This may be because women are now more likely to get a university degree than men are, and because the decline in manufacturing jobs and the 2008 recession both hit men's employment particularly hard.

Keeping up appearances
United States

Share of wives who earn more than their husbands
%

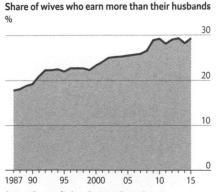

1987 90   95   2000   05   10   15

Sources: Bureau of Labour Statistics; Census Bureau

Difference between stated and actual earnings in couples where wives earn more
2003–13

+2.9% Husbands overstate their salary

Wives understate their salary −1.5%

Women who earn more than their husbands still suffer unwelcome consequences. A study by Marianne Bertrand and Eric Kamenica at the University of Chicago found that such relationships are more likely to end in divorce. The researchers also revealed that when women outearn their husbands, the share of housework they do increases. Another study, by researchers at Cornell University, found that men who earn less than their wives are more likely to be unfaithful (as are those who earn significantly more).

What causes these retrograde patterns? The fact that women who earn more than their husbands take up more housework and under-report their earnings may have to do with the pressure to maintain traditional gender norms: the idea that men should be the primary earners in a family remains deeply ingrained. When men fail to live up to their expected roles, it hurts their self-esteem and social standing. It can also make women lose respect for them. But things may be slowly changing. One study found that the likelihood of divorce did not increase among couples with higher-earning wives who married in the 1990s or later. Researchers at Harvard University have also found that when wives felt that their lower-earning husbands did enough housework, both spouses were more likely to report being happy in their marriage. Perhaps that promises a new definition of actually "manning up".

How the wage penalty for mothers varies from country to country

Germans call them Rabenmütter ("raven mothers") – women who work so hard outside the home that they barely have time for their children. It is meant as an insult. The opposite is a Gluckenmutter ("hen mother"), who dotes on her children as a hen dotes on her eggs. This is hardly complimentary either. Whatever mothers do, it seems, they are expected to feel guilty about it. They also face a wage penalty as soon as they give birth. This is largely because mothers choose to work fewer hours, or in lower-paid but more child-friendly jobs, or not at all when their children are very young. An academic working paper from a multinational group of researchers at the Centre for Economic Policy Research (CEPR), a think-tank, tries to measure this effect. It defines the motherhood penalty as the amount by which women's earnings fall compared with their earnings a year before giving birth. (It includes the non-existent earnings of women who give up work entirely.) It finds that the motherhood penalty exists in all six countries studied – but varies greatly in size.

It was largest in Germany: after ten years, a typical mother was earning 61% less than she was before she gave birth. In Austria the penalty was a still hefty 51%. It was somewhat smaller, at about 40%, in America and Britain, and smallest in Sweden (27%) and Denmark (21%). Men's earnings in all countries were largely unaffected by parenthood. The study found that the motherhood penalty was biggest for mothers whose own mothers had stayed at home when they were children, as these were the most likely to follow their example and also stay at home.

Public policy also accounts for some of the difference. Sweden requires firms to offer 12 months of parental leave per child, split evenly between the two parents, with three months reserved for the father. If he does not take it, it is lost. This is perhaps why Swedish men see a small dip in their earnings after becoming fathers – they take more paternity leave than American or German men do.

Labour costs
Earnings relative to pre-child earnings, 2015 or latest %

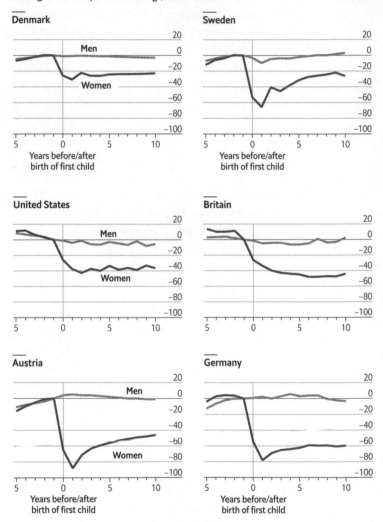

Source: "Child penalties across countries: evidence and explanations",
H. Kleven, C. Landais, J. Posch, A. Steinhauer and J. Zweimüller, CEPR, 2019

However, after three months they tend to go back to work, leaving their wives with the nappies and the carrot-flavoured mush.

The motherhood penalty was largest in countries where more people tell pollsters that women should stay at home with the kids – presumably because in such countries, they are more likely to do so. At the current rate of change, the World Economic Forum estimates that it will be 202 years before men and women achieve parity in the workforce.

How English-speaking proficiency varies from industry to industry

English, non-native speakers are often told, is vital for a high-flying career. Once necessary only for over-achieving, globe-trotting professionals, fluency in the modern lingua franca is now required for a wide range of jobs. Yet the proficiency of people who use English as a second language differs substantially by country and industry.

A report from EF Education First, a language school, attempts to measure these differences. EF's English-speaking proficiency index uses test-score data from 1.3m non-native English speakers across 88 countries who have been assessed using its software. The index equally weights reading and listening tasks to classify test-takers' English-language abilities on a scale from zero to 100.

Between 2016 and 2018 the EF index shows that the English-speaking abilities of test-takers have improved little in two years. Yet it is the differences between industries that are most striking. The gap between proficiency in the highest-ranked fields, such as

---

Lost in translation
English proficiency score* (100=best), by selected industry, 2018

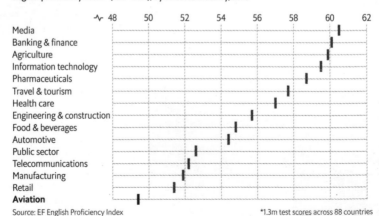

Source: EF English Proficiency Index   *1.3m test scores across 88 countries

media and finance, and in the lowest, such as retail and aviation, stands at a full ten points.

In most industries English-language skills are not a matter of life and death. This cannot be said of aviation. Nonetheless, pilots come in at a lowly seventh among the ten listed aviation job categories. Their average test scores were some 2.5 points below that of marketeers, the best performers, in 2016. Cabin crew fare the worst by far, while air-traffic controllers perform somewhat better than engineers.

How have pilots managed to slip under the radar? The International Civil Aviation Organisation recommends using "aviation English" as the standardised language, employing set phrases and protocols in the hope of preventing miscommunication and accidents. However, aviation English has not been adopted as an official standard, and tests are not compulsory. In 1996 two planes crashed in mid-air near Delhi, India, after one of the pilots, a non-native English speaker, failed to understand instructions regarding his plane's flight level.

How many hours do teachers work around the world?

Few people go into teaching for the money. In most countries, teachers earn less than similarly well-educated workers in other professions. Various reasons are suggested for this, such as job security, parent-friendly working hours and generous pensions. Another possible reason is the workload: the last lesson of the day often ends by mid-afternoon and teachers benefit from the long holidays granted to their students. However, they must also toil outside the classroom, preparing lessons, marking homework and being harangued by pushy parents. In a survey across 35 countries conducted by the Varkey Foundation, an education charity that favours higher status for teachers, the average respondent among 35,000 adults estimated that teachers worked 39 hours per week. Yet the average teacher among 5,500 surveyed claimed to work 43.

Despite underestimating teachers' workload, people still think they are underpaid. In 28 of the 35 countries surveyed, teachers make less than the public deems fair. The average respondent said that a fair wage would be 31% more than teachers actually earn. However, not everyone who tells a pollster that pedagogues should be more generously paid will vote for higher taxes to make that easier. Nor will many parents cheer the idea of larger classes, which would also make it easier to pay teachers more.

What's a teacher worth?
Global Teacher Status Index, 2018

Teachers' working hours
Weekly

▌ General public's perception
▌ Self-reported

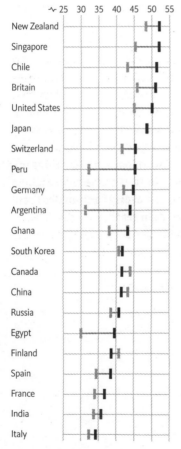

Secondary-school teachers' starting salary, $'000*

General public's ▌ estimate   ▌ perceived fair salary
▌ Actual

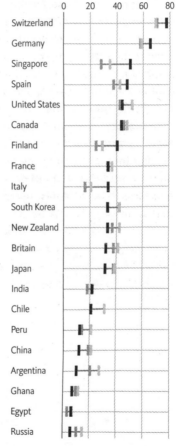

Source: Global Teacher Status Index, 2018

*Purchasing-power parity adjusted

Why do some countries work longer hours than others?

The fall in the number of hours worked per person is among the least-sung benefits of economic development. In the late 19th century, workers in industrialised economies knew labour and little else. In 1870 full-time work generally meant between 60 and 70 hours of labour per week, or more than 3,000 hours per year. Over the century that followed, rising incomes were accompanied by a steady drop in weekly hours, which had fallen to about 40, on average, by 1970. Though less conspicuous a boon than larger pay packets or higher living standards, the drop was a gift to working people of a thousand or so precious hours of free time each year.

Hours worked are hard to measure. But the best analyses suggest that such gifts have been far less generous in the years since, in some countries at least. In France and Germany hours worked per person have continued to drop over the past few decades, albeit more slowly than in the past. In Germany, where one of the largest trade unions won the right to a 28-hour working week for

---

Punching the clock
Annual hours worked per worker, '000

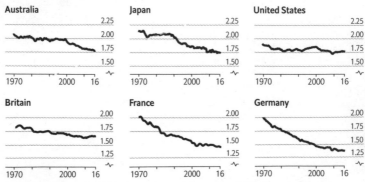

Source: "Aggregate hours worked in OECD countries: new measurement and implications for business cycles", L. Ohanian and A. Raffo, *Journal of Monetary Economics*

its workers in 2018, employees now put in fewer than 1,400 hours per year. The decline in America and Britain has been substantially smaller; indeed, hours worked in those countries have actually risen since the 2000s.

Why should time spent in work vary so much? Analyses of differences between countries focus on culture: of course leisure-loving Europeans put in fewer hours than puritanical Americans and striving South Koreans. Such explanations are unsatisfying, however. Italians and Greeks work many more hours than their supposedly more diligent northern neighbours, for instance. Economists, for their part, often think about the choice to work more or fewer hours in terms of competing "substitution" and "income" effects. Forces that increase the returns earned from working (such as reductions in marginal tax rates or higher pay) make each hour of work more lucrative, and can therefore cause workers to choose to work more: to substitute working hours for leisure time. That said, when people are richer they tend to consume more of the things they enjoy, including leisure. So a higher effective return to work, by raising income, can also lead to a decline.

Why Japan is accepting more foreign workers

Foreign cashiers and carers are now a fact of life in Japan, especially in urban areas. The number of foreign workers has risen fast recently, to 1.3m – some 2% of the workforce. Although visas that allow foreigners to settle in Japan are in theory mainly for highly skilled workers, in practice those with fewer skills may be admitted as students or trainees or as immigrants of Japanese extraction. In June 2018 the government announced that it would create a "designated-skills" visa in order to bring in 500,000 new workers by 2025, in agriculture, construction, hotels, nursing and shipbuilding.

Japan has historically been wary of admitting foreigners. It is one of the rich world's most homogenous countries: just 2% of residents are foreigners, compared with 4% in South Korea and 16% in France. The reasons for this attitude range from fears that outsiders will bring crime and damage societal practices, to concerns that Japanese residents will not be able to communicate properly with them. But Japan's population is old and getting smaller. To fill shortages in the labour force caused by the shrinking working-age population, government policy has focused on getting more women and old people into work, and using robots and artificial intelligence. It has become apparent, however, that this is not enough. Businesses also want foreigners to help them remain competitive and to become more global.

And pressure from business is a big reason behind the government's change of tack. Over the past 20 years the number of workers under 30 has shrunk by a quarter. Another result of the greying population is the creation of ever more jobs, most notably as carers, that few Japanese want to do at the wages on offer. There are 60% more job vacancies than there are people looking for work. Industries such as agriculture and construction, as well as nursing, are increasingly dependent on foreigners. More exposure to foreigners, through a boom in tourism, has reassured Japanese, especially the young, that they can get along with them.

poll conducted in 2017 found opinion evenly split about whether

Japan should admit more foreign workers, with 42% agreeing and 42% disagreeing. Some 60% of 18- to 29-year-olds were in favour, however, which was double the share among the over-70s.

Attracting the foreign workers Japan needs will not necessarily be easy. Language is a big barrier. Japanese-language abilities are not necessary for highly skilled workers wanting visas, but only a handful of companies work in English. Lowlier workers, who must pass a Japanese exam, are currently not allowed to bring their families and will not be able to under the "designated-skills" visa. Firms in which promotion is based on seniority rather than merit, and in which long hours are the norm, will find it hard to attract workers. Japan also needs to do more to help integrate foreigners. By accepting, for the most part, a small number of highly skilled workers, Japan has been able to get away without any integration policy. But as the number of immigrants rises, and especially as more low-skilled workers are admitted, this omission threatens to bring about some of the very concerns, such as poverty and a failure to integrate into society, that prompted the government to restrict immigration in the first place.

The slow progress towards gender parity in the sciences

"Physics was invented and built by men, it's not by invitation," said Alessandro Strumia at CERN, Europe's nuclear-research centre, in September 2018. The Italian physicist went on to reveal plenty more tone-deaf and sexist views (at a colloquium on gender and physics, no less) before being summarily suspended.

There is, alas, a nugget of insight in Dr Strumia's comment. Physics, and the rest of the physical sciences, started as all-male affairs and most sub-disciplines remain male-dominated even today. Achieving gender parity in the higher echelons of research, where Nobel-worthy work gets done, remains a distant challenge. That there have been fewer Nobel prizes awarded to female scientists is therefore, in part, an issue of demographics and history: the prizes are often given for work done decades previously, when gender imbalances were even more pronounced.

That said, the proportion of science Nobels given to women remains woeful. Donna Strickland, one of 2018's physics laureates,

Science friction

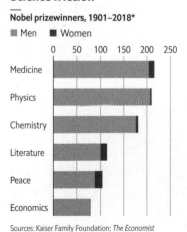

Nobel prizewinners, 1901–2018*

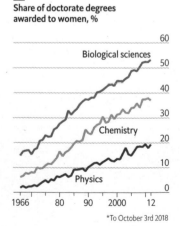

Share of doctorate degrees awarded to women, %

Sources: Kaiser Family Foundation; *The Economist*   *To October 3rd 2018

was the first woman to receive the prize in 55 years, and only the third in the prize's history. The Nobel Foundation has at last taken the issue in hand, and from 2019 the scientists who suggest contenders will be specifically encouraged to nominate female scientists; half of the prize committees themselves are now led by women. Increasingly, physics and the sciences more broadly are being built by women, no invitation required. Honouring them with a fair share of science's biggest accolades, it is hoped, will just be a matter of time.

How NFL contracts give players so little power

In America the rules of the National Football League (NFL), the National Basketball Association (NBA), the National Hockey League (NHL) and Major League Baseball (MLB) all allow players to be traded without their consent to organisations on the other side of the country. At their new club they will usually retain the terms and length of their original deal. But of the four leagues, it is the NFL that gives players the least power and security over their contracts. Why?

Unlike those of the NBA, NHL and MLB, the vast majority of the NFL's player contracts are not actually "guaranteed". They confirm neither the identity of a player's employer nor his pay. The contract's headline value is heavily dependent on the player fulfilling the terms of clauses relating to performance, or on the organisation deciding they want to keep him. NFL stars can be released from their contracts if they are injured or performing poorly, and their employers do not have to pay out the full value of the deals. For example, in 2010 Donovan McNabb signed a five-year contract extension with the Washington Redskins worth $78m. But it was reported that nothing beyond $3.5m in the first season was guaranteed. The Redskins had an option on whether to activate the remaining four years of the deal, but never did so. Mr McNabb was traded to the Minnesota Vikings in 2011 after underwhelming performances, and was released by Minnesota later that year, having received a fraction of the value of the deal he signed in 2010.

There is no legal reason why NFL deals should not be fully guaranteed. But team owners have little incentive to change a situation that works in their favour, as they would if they were to rewrite the current collective bargaining agreement (CBA), a labour agreement between players and owners. One reason why owners hesitate to guarantee money is that the CBA requires teams to put any guaranteed money in escrow at the time of a contract's signing, even if it is not due to be paid for years. Another is the NFL's salary cap. Russell Okung, who plays for the Los Angeles Chargers, argued in July 2018 that owners hesitate to guarantee money because of the way portions of a team's salary cap can be locked up in "dead money". This is money guaranteed to a player when a contract is signed, which counts as part of the team's salary payments for the whole of the deal, even if that player has been released. "Dead money" hurts a team's ability to spend in future. The majority of player incomes are therefore only guaranteed from one year to the next – a particular worry in a game with a high risk of injury. A paper published under Harvard University's Football Players Health Study estimated that, on average, NFL games see five times as many injuries as the sum of injuries in the other three leagues.

The current CBA expires in 2021, and renegotiation will be a battle between the interests of players and owners. Todd Gurley, a running-back for the Los Angeles Rams, said that players may have to strike to advance their cause. Le'Veon Bell's decision to sit out games for the Pittsburgh Steelers in the 2018 season, in hopes of obtaining more guaranteed money in a contract extension, looks a harbinger of labour conflicts to come. There have been some positive signs for players. Kirk Cousins signed a three year, fully guaranteed deal worth $84m with the Minnesota Vikings – the first deal of its kind. But such a contract is an anomaly reserved for the game's top few, and owners still have little incentive to change the structure. For the vast majority of those who play in the NFL, contract security will remain a rarity.

Why star football managers make less difference than star players

"I think I am a special one," José Mourinho boasted in 2004. One of football's most lauded managers, he won six domestic titles in his first 11 seasons in top leagues. But his powers have deserted him of late. He was sacked by Chelsea in 2015, and by Manchester United in 2018. Fans lay most of the credit or blame for their team's results on the manager. So do executives: nearly half of clubs in top leagues changed coach in 2018. Yet this faith appears misplaced. After analysing 15 years of league data, *The Economist* found that an overachieving manager's odds of sustaining that success in a new job are barely better than a coin flip. The likely cause of the "decline" of once-feted bosses like Mr Mourinho is not that they lose their touch, but that their early wins owe more to players and luck than to their own wizardry.

A manager's impact is hard to gauge. So how should credit be split between the boss and his charges? To separate their effects, we needed a measure of players' skill. We found it in an unlikely place: video games. Electronic Arts' "FIFA" series rates 18,000 players each year, based on their statistics and subjective reports from 9,000 fans. These scores yield reliable match forecasts. Using only pre-season FIFA ratings, we could predict the final table with an average error of eight league points. By comparing actual results with these projections, we could see which clubs did better than their players' ratings implied. Teams do over-perform for reasons other than their managers. But if coaching matters, the best bosses should continue to exceed expectations when they switch clubs.

And managers do carry over some impact. However, the effect is small. For a manager switching jobs after one year, we expect his new team to reap just 8% of his prior outperformance. Even after a decade of coaching, this figure is still only 45%, implying that the primary causes of a manager's previous successes were beyond his control. A few bosses have beaten expectations for long enough to deserve proper credit. Despite lacking the star power of La Liga's

Star managers don't improve teams as much as star players do

Distribution of managers and players*
from "big five" leagues†, 2004–18

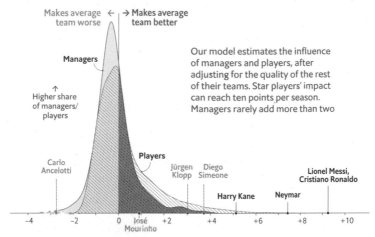

Makes average ← | → Makes average
team worse | team better

Managers

↑
Higher share
of managers/
players

Our model estimates the influence
of managers and players, after
adjusting for the quality of the rest
of their teams. Star players' impact
can reach ten points per season.
Managers rarely add more than two

Carlo
Ancelotti

Players

Jürgen   Diego
Klopp   Simeone

Harry Kane   Neymar

Lionel Messi,
Cristiano Ronaldo

-4   -2   0   José   +2   +4   +6   +8   +10
                Mourinho

Expected league points per season gained/lost

Over/underperformance in consecutive jobs
For every 100 managers‡, after adjusting for players' skill

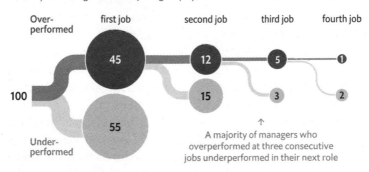

Over-
performed

first job

second job

third job

fourth job

45

12

5

❶

100

15

3

2

55

Under-
performed

↑
A majority of managers who
overperformed at three consecutive
jobs underperformed in their next role

Sources: Electronic Arts; Transfermarkt   *Each team's best 13 players
†England, France, Germany, Italy and Spain   ‡Tenures of at least 15 games

titans, Diego Simeone led Atlético Madrid to a Spanish title. And Jürgen Klopp turned mid-table Borussia Dortmund into two-time German champions.

Conversely, our analysis (carried out in January 2019) found that Carlo Ancelotti had squandered resources. Although he led the team with the best players in its league in eight of his previous 12 seasons, he won only three titles in that time. A top-league player who fared so poorly would have lost his job. But the market for coaches is inefficient. Mr Ancelotti keeps getting hired – perhaps because employers over-weight his three Champions League trophies, which required a much smaller number of wins. Even the best tacticians cannot compete with those who contribute with their feet. Mr Simeone would improve an average club by four points, similar to the 50th-best player in the world. But greats like Lionel Messi can add twice as much or more.

By the numbers: economical, with the truth

What's in it for the Belt-and-Road countries?

In the days when the Silk Road linked China to Europe, merchants would crisscross Eurasia, stopping at the caravanserais (roadside inns) that had sprouted up across Central Asia and the southern Caucasus. But as trade came to rely more on shipping, land routes fell out of favour and many Eurasian hubs floundered. A stream of projects launched in 2013 by the Chinese president, Xi Jinping, may change that. The so-called "Belt and Road Initiative" (BRI) aims to improve trading and transport links between China and the world, mostly through infrastructure investments. It promises to revive the fortunes of ex-Soviet states of Central Asia. But what do these countries stand to gain from a flow of what will be predominantly Chinese goods?

The scale of the initiative is enormous. So far China is estimated to have underwritten over $900bn of loans – some on concessionary terms, many on commercial terms – in 71 countries, ranging from Poland to Pakistan. Many projects are under way. Kazakhstan has opened a massive dry port on its eastern border with China. Its seaports on the Caspian sea are also being expanded, and east-west rail and road connections are being upgraded. On the other side of the Caspian, Azerbaijan and Georgia hope to capture some of the flow of Chinese goods to Europe via the Baku-Tbilisi-Kars railway, which opened in 2017, and Georgia has secured $50m in Chinese investment in a proposed deep-sea port on the Black Sea. Other countries are jockeying to attract Chinese attention for BRI projects. In November 2017 the Georgian government held its second biennial Tbilisi Belt and Road Forum, in which delegations from Europe, the Middle East and Central Asia presented historical trade route maps as part of their efforts to earn a place on this 21st-century Silk Road, with all the accompanying Chinese investment.

Underlying such machinations lies the assumption that the BRI will deliver a host of lucrative spillover effects to the transit countries. Many have underdeveloped or poorly maintained infrastructure. The economic benefits of a new motorway, railway or port for the hospitality, industrial or retail sectors seem clear enough. Such developments should make trading between neighbours easier – something that Kazakhstan and Uzbekistan have already been taking advantage of. And governments like to take credit for shiny new infrastructure projects without having to raise revenue to pay for them or subject themselves to conditions set by Western investors or multilateral organisations.

But worries persist. China supplies the workers to implement the projects, limiting the scope for local involvement. Transit countries are likely to keep trade tariffs to a minimum to discourage China from using different, cheaper routes for its goods – but this limits opportunities to raise revenue. BRI countries claim that their nascent manufacturing industries can be integrated into the Chinese value chain so that, for example, machine parts made in China could be assembled in Kazakhstan. But manufacturing sectors across the former Soviet Union are uncompetitive and businesses complain of shortages of skilled labour. Most worryingly, perhaps, countries along the route are already heavily indebted. If the returns on BRI investment prove underwhelming, they could struggle to repay China's loans and to pay for maintenance, causing bilateral relations to sour. As a result, this modern Silk Road may end up being less renowned for the spread of prosperity than its historical forebear.

What is sustainable finance?

Traditionally, investors evaluated their performance based on financial measures alone. But investing with an eye to environmental or social issues, not just financial returns, has become mainstream in the past decade. According to the Global Sustainable Investment Alliance (GSIA), an umbrella group, fully $23trn, or 26% of all assets under management in 2016, were in "socially responsible investments" that take account of environmental, social and governance (ESG) issues. But what counts as "sustainable investment" in the first place?

The nascent space still suffers from definitional quibbles: both over where to draw the line between sustainable and "normal" investments, and how to subdivide the universe of sustainable investment. The GSIA, for instance, counts seven distinct strategies. The least involved variant, and the one accounting for the greatest share of assets under management – around $15trn in 2016 – is "negative screening", which simply excludes assets deemed unsavoury. An example would be a stock portfolio that otherwise tracks a broad index, but excludes the shares of tobacco companies or arms manufacturers. "ESG integration", the second-largest category by the GSIA's reckoning, involves taking ESG factors into account in the investment process, though the way investment firms do this in practice varies widely. Of the remaining strategies, perhaps the most interesting is "impact investment", which has received a lot of attention recently. Although it is the smallest by assets, it is also by far the most ambitious. Impact investors only invest in projects or firms where the precise impact can be quantified and measured: for instance, the reduction in tonnes of carbon dioxide emitted by a firm's factory, or the number of girls educated in a village school as a result of a particular project. These variants are quite different but most are set up on the premise that financial return need not be sacrificed in pursuit of non-financial goals.

As demand has broadened from rich individuals to institutional investors, mainstream financial firms have entered the space.

Investors seeking ESG investment options can turn to BlackRock, the world's largest asset manager, or the asset-management division of Goldman Sachs, a bank. Impact-investment firms used to be small and niche, but two of America's largest private-equity firms, Bain Capital and TPG, have launched such funds. Offerings are available across asset classes, too. Bond investors can turn to a whole new asset class, that of "green bonds", the proceeds of which are earmarked for environmental projects. (Issuance of such bonds rocketed from less than \$500m in 2008 to over \$160bn in 2017.)

Consistent measures and ratings are still a work in progress. For instance, many data providers now rate companies on ESG metrics, allowing investors to compare companies easily. Issuers of green bonds have long sought external validation of their environmental credentials. While the first certification schemes merely made a binary ruling on whether bonds were green or not, new methodologies seek to quantify the relative environmental impact. Measures that allow for comparison across investments are still lacking. The European Union wants to change that, and has announced plans to set up an overarching framework for evaluating ESG ratings (ie, a way to rate ratings, not just another ratings system). But the more fundamental question is the trickiest to solve, because it boils down to ethics rather than finance. How can the relative value of, say, educating a girl in the developing world be compared with preventing a tonne of air pollution? In the end, investors' choices among the different variants of sustainable investments will be driven by their own personal interests, rather than just by financial calculations.

How to do the most good possible

Imagine you are walking in a park and come across a boy drowning in a pond. Chances are, you would not hesitate to jump in to save him, even if it meant ruining an expensive pair of shoes. Yet, if you read a news report about thousands of children drowning because of a flood in a distant country, you might not feel compelled to act at all. What could explain this seemingly incongruous gap in empathy? One reason is that you, as a human, are simply hard-wired to care more about those in your immediate vicinity. But another is that you might believe that you have no ability to meaningfully affect the lives of distant strangers. Members of the "effective altruism" movement, a group of scientifically minded do-gooders, argue that this view is too pessimistic. They reckon that social science has advanced to the point where it is possible for individuals to do a tangible amount of good.

The most obvious way to affect the world is to choose the right career. Teaching is considered a natural vocation for a would-be do-gooder, but it is not clear that it should be. Effective altruists argue that if you are choosing a career and want to help the world, you should not worry about how much good a profession does overall – rather, you should focus on the impact you would make if you join it. If you become a teacher, the chances are you would not actually increase the total number of teachers in your country. Instead, you would simply be taking a spot away from another candidate with a CV that looks a lot like yours. A better option might be to get a job on Wall Street. If you become a derivatives trader and commit to giving a large portion of your salary to charity, you might make a very positive impact on the world, because you would be taking a job away from someone who would probably not donate the same amount of money.

One of the biggest intellectual achievements of the effective-altruism movement has been the emergence of schemes for charity evaluation. GiveWell, a non-profit firm, has taken research from development economics and used it to calculate how much good each dollar donated to a number of charities can do. It measures a charity's success not in financial returns, but rather by factors such as how much it costs the charity to save a life. For example, the Against Malaria Foundation distributes anti-malarial bed nets in sub-Saharan Africa. GiveWell reckons that the benefits of its work add up to the equivalent of a life saved for every $2,000 spent by donors. A typical household in America makes around $58,000 a year. Suppose it commits 10% of that, every year, to efficient charities. Over the course of a 40-year working life, this would add up to $232,000. GiveWell's analysis implies that such a family would be responsible for saving the lives of 116 children if it were to give to the Against Malaria Foundation. Similar analyses can be applied to other charities, allowing donors to assess the impact of their altruism and maximise whatever metric is most important to them.

Peter Singer, an Australian philosopher who first came up with the drowning-child argument, notes that the efficiency of the charity to which one gives is as important as the amount given. This is true for many causes. For instance, if you are interested in maximising the public enjoyment of art, you could choose to buy an expensive picture for a museum. Or you could spend just $100 and help someone living in a poor country get surgery to prevent blindness from trachoma. They could then spend their entire life gazing upon paintings. Effective altruism can be a hard sell, even for the rationally minded. Those from Silicon Valley have been keener to embrace the philosophy than those working on Wall Street, for instance. Effective altruists fret that their movement might, in fact, have very limited appeal. Utility-maximising automatons might see the sense in buying mosquito nets for distant strangers. But human beings might find, say, volunteering at a local soup kitchen more satisfying emotionally.

Why fewer people are using public transport

In much of the rich world, urban public transport is becoming quieter. New York's subway carried 2% fewer people on weekdays from mid-2017 to mid-2018 than it did in the previous 12 months, and the city's buses were 6% less busy. London's "Tube" dipped unexpectedly, too. This is a puzzle. After all, most large cities are growing in population. Employment is often rising even more quickly. Urbanites have jobs to go to – and, because they have jobs, money to spend in shops and restaurants. But they are not taking trains or buses as much as they used to.

Cities have noticed the trend, and they have plenty of excuses for it. Some point out that service levels on public transport have worsened. Delays are up in some cities, either because too little is being spent on public transport or because (in New York, for example) it is being spent on beautiful stations rather than on signals that work. Others say that buses are being slowed by roadworks, making them less appealing. A few cities, such as Paris, have suffered terrorist attacks, which may have scared people off public transport. In still others, ticket prices have risen.

These excuses are probably not enough to explain a widespread decline. Even in cities where public transport is much better than it was (Los Angeles, for example) passenger numbers have slumped. It seems more likely that public transport is being squeezed structurally, from two directions. First, people's need to travel is diminishing as a result of smartphones, video-conferencing, online shopping and so on. Second, urbanites now have more and better options for getting around. Uber is already ubiquitous, and several city-level studies suggest that ride-hailing seems to be discouraging the use of public transport. Easy-to-rent dockless bicycles are spreading; battery-powered scooters are next. When driverless taxis appear in cities, as they eventually should, public transport may come to seem even less appealing. For now, driving is easier than it used to be because car loans have become so cheap.

Public transport is in some ways the opposite of driving. When more people drive, the roads become clogged, delays go up, and driving becomes less appealing. When more people use buses or trains, by contrast, the service usually improves because public-transport agencies run more buses and trains. Until recently, many wealthy cities were in that happy loop. Now the pattern has reversed. If the decline in passengers continues, cities could be pulled into a downward spiral of fewer passengers and worse service. Some of the shine has already come off public transport. In May 2018, voters in Nashville overwhelmingly rejected a plan to raise taxes to pay for a larger public-transport system. Opponents of the scheme had not only argued (as opponents usually do) that new taxes are bad. They had also asserted that public transport is outmoded. The future, apparently, is driverless cars.

Do "sin taxes" actually work?

Tobacco was new to England in the 17th century, but even then, smoking had plenty of critics. The most famous was King James I, who in 1604 described smoking as "a custome lothsome to the eye, hatefull to the Nose, harmful to the braine, dangerous to the Lungs, and in the blacke and stinking fume thereof, nearest resembling the Stigian smoke of the pit that is bottomless". The king increased the import tax on the "noxious weed" by 4,000%. There are several justifications for imposing a tax on a specific product. One is that it raises money for the government. A second, which only applies to a small subset of products, is that its use inflicts costs on third parties that are not factored into its price. A textbook example of such "negative externalities" is air pollution. Without intervention from the government, the economy will produce too many goods that foul up the atmosphere. That benefits manufacturers and consumers, but harms everyone who breathes in the by-products.

"Sin taxes" apply this logic to goods deemed to be socially undesirable. Proponents of such taxes argue that because activities like smoking are unhealthy, smokers should pay additional taxes to compensate the government for the additional spending on medical care that their habit will one day cost the treasury. However, many studies overstate the magnitude of such externalities, because they present gross costs instead of net ones. There is no doubt that smokers, alcoholics and the obese receive a disproportionately high share of public spending on health while they are alive. But they also tend to die unusually young. That reduces the amount the government must spend on their pensions. Moreover, people who abstain from unhealthy practices also get sick and die eventually. Sooner or later, they will cost public-health systems money as well. The Institute of Economic Affairs, a conservative think-tank, finds that after accounting for sin taxes, welfare costs, crime and early deaths, tobacco and alcohol actually save the British government £14.7bn ($18.7bn) and £6.5bn a year respectively. In contrast, obesity costs it £2.5bn per year.

Deterrent effects

United States, estimated fall in sales
associated with a 1% increase in price, %

Britain, annual cost to government
of vices, 2017 or latest available, £bn

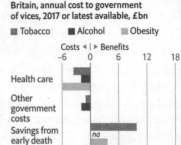

Sources: IFS; academic studies; Institute of Economic Affairs

A third rationale for imposing sin taxes, beyond raising revenue and compensating society for the harm caused by the use of certain products, is to discourage individuals from consuming them in the first place. Critics of such taxes argue that this approach tends to be ineffective because the goods targeted tend to be addictive, which makes consumers relatively unresponsive to changes in price. In fact, study after study has shown that sin taxes do tend to reduce consumption. Nevertheless, as policy instruments, sin taxes are extremely blunt. People who drink or smoke only occasionally do their bodies little harm and impose few costs on the rest of society, yet are taxed no differently from heavy smokers and drinkers. A study published in 2017 by the Institute for Fiscal Studies (IFS), a think-tank, found that Britons who bought only a few drinks a week were far more sensitive to price fluctuations than heavy drinkers. The IFS suggests that it might make more sense to place higher levies on the tipples more in favour with heavy drinkers, such as spirits.

The point of sin taxes is to make unhealthy goods more expensive on a relative basis, not to make the poor poorer. So a further concern is that they affect low-income households most. In theory, the sin taxes could be offset by earmarking any revenue from them for direct cash transfers or for social programmes aimed at reducing poverty. Philadelphia, for example, has earmarked the revenue from its sugar tax for schools, parks and libraries. The best argument for sin taxes is the behavioural one. Economic models assume that people know what they are doing. Flesh-and-blood humans struggle with self-control. Most smokers are well aware of the health risks, but many still find it hard to quit. Tax policy can help. Once you allow for even a sliver of irrationality in human decision-making, the case for taxing addictive substances becomes clear. In America, heart disease is linked to one in four deaths, and smoking to one in five. Sin taxes work, in the sense that they can make people healthier. But since most of the damage smokers, drinkers and the obese do is to themselves, rather than to others, governments need to think carefully about how much they want to interfere. And any cost-benefit analysis on the social impact of these vices needs to take into account that people do find them enjoyable. There is more to life than living longer.

Why tariffs are bad taxes

President Donald Trump has called tariffs "the greatest!" He is deploying them liberally, slapping new ones on imports that were worth $89bn in 2017. Sometimes he talks of tariffs as tools to bully others into taking down trade barriers of their own. At other times he seems keen to protect American industries from competition that he perceives to be unfair. And he likes the resulting revenue. So why are economists upset by his enthusiasm for tariffs?

Tariffs are taxes which create a wedge between the price paid by buyers of imported goods and the price foreign sellers get. Narrow tariffs aimed at specific products, such as cars, nudge consumers towards home-made goods and away from imports they might otherwise prefer. (Broader tariffs covering a large share of imports are more complicated, as exchange rates can move to offset some of their effects.) Tariffs resemble sales taxes in that they discourage some exchanges that may be mutually beneficial for both parties. But unlike sales taxes, they discriminate between products based on where they are made. They are fiddlier too: different rates apply to thousands of different products. And they encourage lobbying by powerful industries seeking protection.

And although they raise revenue for the government, tariffs impose costs on the country setting them. They invite foreigners to respond with retaliatory tariffs of their own, hurting exporters. (When new tariffs break past promises, they also erode trust.) Moreover, tariffs distort the economy, reducing productivity. Though monetary and fiscal policy can keep overall employment relatively stable regardless of trade patterns, discriminatory duties can rebalance the economy towards protected industries, drawing workers and investment away from others. No doubt some American steel-company executives were pleased with Mr Trump's 25% tariff on imported steel. But domestic companies that buy steel to make higher-value products were miffed.

There are some arguments in favour of tariffs. In poor countries they can be easier to collect than sales taxes, requiring only

Withdrawal symptoms

% change following a one percentage point increase in tariff rate

Output

Productivity

Trade balance

Years after rate change

Source: "Macroeconomic consequences of tariffs", D. Furceri, S. A. Hannan, J. D. Ostry and A. K. Rose, National Bureau of Economic Research, 2018

infrastructure at ports. Provisions allowing countries to impose new ones help garner political support for free-trade deals and act as a safety valve in case of a disruptive surge of imports. And it may be that in some circumstances, tariffs can help an industry catch up with foreign competitors by offering temporary relief from more developed rivals. But well-meaning protectionists should take note. Muffled beneath the hurrahs of a small number of winners from tariffs are the harrumphs of a much larger base of quiet losers – including other businesses, entrepreneurs and consumers, all of whom end up paying more.

How Venezuela's hyperinflation compares with previous examples

For those not enduring it, hyperinflation can seem mind-bendingly abstract. In Venezuela's faltering economy, prices rose by 223.1% in August 2018 alone, according to Ángel Alvarado, an economist and opposition politician (the government has long ceased publishing official statistics). Inflation was expected to reach 1m% for the full year, according to a (somewhat loose) forecast by the IMF. Such a figure is far from unprecedented, however. In the worst month of its post-war hyperinflation, Hungarian prices rose by 41,900,000,000,000,000%. The government had to print a 100 quintillion note (with 20 zeroes), the highest denomination banknote ever produced.

Venezuela's hyperinflation in 2018 ranks only 23rd out of the 57 episodes identified by Steve Hanke of Johns Hopkins University and Nicholas Krus, an independent economist. To make the numbers easier to grasp, and episodes easier to compare, the two economists calculated how long it would have taken for prices to double, if inflation persisted at its peak monthly pace. Their results provide a kind of "half-life" for a currency, showing in each case how long it took for it to lose 50% of its value (relative to the country's consumer goods and services).

This alternative approach turns the astronomical percentages of

Runaway reaction
Hyperinflation, number of days for prices to double at peak monthly rate

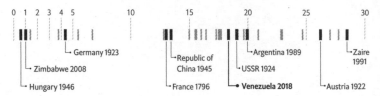

Sources: "World hyperinflations", S. H. Hanke and N. Krus, CATO Working Paper, 2012; *The Economist*

hyperinflation into more mundane intervals of time: millions into days and quintillions into hours. In Venezuela's case it took less than 19 days in August 2018 for the currency to lose half its value. But in the worst month of Hungary's hyperinflation, it took just 15 hours.

How big companies are making markets less competitive

Since 1978 total corporate profits in America have risen from 1.9% of GDP to 4.5%. Although this increase has delivered a windfall for shareholders, it may reflect less dynamism in important sectors of the economy. Three different statistical measures suggest that there is cause for concern.

Take concentration first. The numbers need to be treated with caution, but between 1997 and 2012 concentration rose in two-thirds of 900-odd census industries, with the weighted average market share of the top four firms growing from 26% to 32%. It continued to rise in 2012–14. A tenth of the economy is made up of industries where four firms have more than two-thirds of the market.

Profits are abnormally high as well. A good measure is the free cashflow of corporate firms. This is 76% above its 50-year average, relative to GDP. There are pockets where profits and prices are high compared with other countries, including airlines, credit cards, telecoms, pharmaceutical distribution and credit checking. As anyone who has squeezed into an old economy-class seat or signed fiddly receipts at the check-out knows, these industries clearly lag behind the rest of the world. They also involve thickets of regulation.

As for openness, America is still the world's largest centre of innovation. It spends $450bn a year on R&D, 20% more than China and more than Europe, Japan and South Korea combined. But business churn is subdued: of the listed firms that made a very high return in 1997, 50% still did in 2017 (using a hurdle of 15% and excluding goodwill). Fewer new firms are being started. And America's opening up to the world has stalled, with the value of trade-to-GDP falling steadily since 2011 and the output of foreign firms' subsidiaries in America stagnating.

Europe's leading firms tend to be smaller and more internationally oriented than their American counterparts. Nonetheless, concentration is creeping up in Europe as well. A study by Chiara Criscuolo and colleagues at the OECD, a club of

Monopoly money

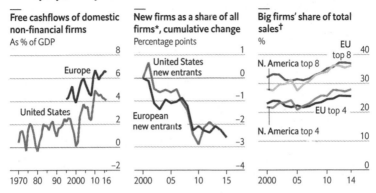

Free cashflows of domestic non-financial firms
As % of GDP

New firms as a share of all firms*, cumulative change
Percentage points

Big firms' share of total sales†
%

Sources: OECD and *Economist* estimates; "Declining business dynamism; evidence and causes", F. Calvino, C. Criscuolo and R. Verlhac, OECD; "Industry concentration in Europe and North America", M. Bajgar, G. Berlingieri, S. Calligaris, C. Criscuolo and J. Timmis, OECD

*Average of countries and industries
†Average of all industries

mainly rich countries, shows that the average market share of the top four firms in each industry has risen by three percentage points since 2000, roughly half of the rise in North America. The free cashflow of non-financial firms as a share of GDP is 18% above its 20-year average. A very profitable listed firm in 1997 had a 46% chance of still being very profitable in 2017. Like America, Europe has suffered a decline in the number of new firms. It is weak on innovation, spending half as much on R&D in absolute terms as America. It scores better on trade, however, which has risen slightly relative to GDP since 2007. But in both Europe and America the trend towards greater concentration and less competition is clear.

Why economics is the most rational choice of subject at Oxbridge

Sceptics of higher education often complain that universities offer too many frivolous degrees with little value in the workplace. Because elite universities tend to produce higher-earning graduates than less selective institutions do, you might expect them to teach more practical courses. Yet data from Britain's department for education show the opposite. Undergraduate students at prestigious universities are more likely to study purely academic fields such as philosophy and classics, whereas those at less choosy ones tend to pick vocational topics such as business or nursing. What could explain this seeming contradiction?

One reason is that employers treat a degree from a top university as a proxy for intelligence. This means students at elite institutions can study bookish subjects and still prosper financially. The median Cambridge graduate in a creative-arts subject – the university's least lucrative group of courses, including fields such as music – earns around £25,000 ($32,000) at age 26. Economics students from less exalted universities, such as Hull, make a similar amount. Yet even though Oxbridge students can pretend to read "Ulysses" for years and still expect a decent salary, they end up paying a large opportunity cost by pursuing the arts.

That is because employers reserve the highest starting wages for students who both attended a leading university and also studied a marketable subject. Cambridge creative-arts graduates earn £11,000 more at age 26 than do those from Wrexham Glyndwr University, whose arts alumni are the lowest-earning in Britain. In contrast, Cambridge economics graduates make £44,000 more than those from the University of Salford, where the economics course is the country's least remunerative.

Many gifted arts students would struggle to crunch numbers. But for those who can excel at both, the cost of sticking with the arts, in terms of forgone wages, is steep. Cambridge creative-arts students have A-level scores comparable to those of economics

Relatively few students at Britain's top universities study vocational fields

■ Oxford & Cambridge   ■ Rest of top 20 universities*
▨ All other universities

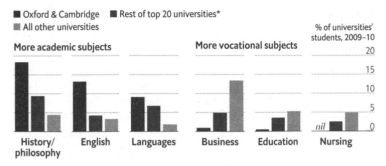

More academic subjects · More vocational subjects · % of universities' students, 2009–10

History/philosophy · English · Languages · Business · Education · Nursing

Graduate earnings vary more by course at higher-ranked universities

Median earnings, 2014–16

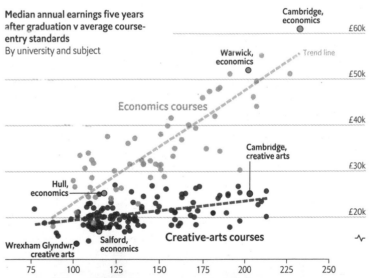

Median annual earnings five years after graduation v average course-entry standards
By university and subject

Average course-entry standards, 2016–17 (three A-grades at both AS- and A-level = 204)

Sources: UCAS; Department for Education

*By UCAS entry standards

students at Warwick University, but earn about half as much. That is tantamount to giving up an annuity worth £500,000. Who can afford such indulgence? The answer is Oxbridge students, who often have rich parents. At most universities, students in courses that lead to high-paying jobs, such as economics and medicine, tend to come from wealthier families, partly because such applicants are more likely to have the examination scores necessary to be accepted. At Oxbridge, however, no such correlation exists. History and philosophy students there come from richer parts of Britain, on average, than their peers studying medicine do. To maximise their earning potential, however, it is clear which subject they ought to pay more attention to: economics.

The Australian economy's remarkable run

Last time Australia suffered a recession, the Soviet Union still existed and the world wide web did not. An American-led force had just liberated Kuwait, and almost half the world's current population had not yet been born. Unlike most of the region, Australia was left unscathed by the Asian crash of 1997. Unlike most of the developed world, it shrugged off the global financial crisis. And unlike most commodity-exporting countries, it weathered the resources bust, too. No other rich country has ever managed to grow so steadily for so long. By that measure, at least, Australia boasts the world's most successful economy.

By other measures, Australia's economic performance is more remarkable still. Whereas many other rich countries have seen wages stagnate for decades, Australia's have grown strongly, albeit less steadily in recent years. In other words, a problem that has agitated policymakers – and voters – around the world, and has been blamed for all manner of political upheaval, from European populism to the election of Donald Trump, scarcely exists in Australia. And that is not the only way in which Australia stands out from its peers. At a time when governments around the world are souring on immigration, and even seeking to send some foreigners home, Australia has been admitting as many as 190,000 newcomers a year – nearly three times as many, relative to population, as America. Population growth has helped underpin economic growth. More than 28% of the population were born in another country, far more than in other rich countries. Half of all living Australians were born abroad or are the child of someone who was.

In part, this tolerance for outsiders may be a reflection of another remarkable feature of Australian society: the solvency of its welfare state. Complaints about foreign spongers are rare. Public debt amounts to just 41% of GDP – one of the lowest levels in the rich world. That, in turn, is a function not only of Australia's enviable record in terms of growth, but also of a history of shrewd policymaking. Some 30 years ago, the government of the day

Dinkum income

1991=100 ━━ **Australia** ━━ United States ━━ Canada, Britain, Germany, Japan and France

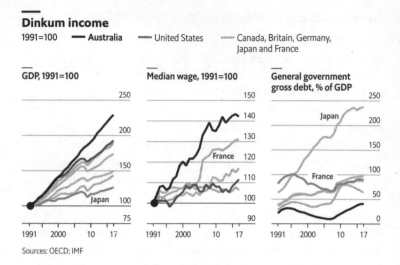

GDP, 1991=100

Median wage, 1991=100

General government gross debt, % of GDP

Sources: OECD; IMF

overhauled the pension system. Since then workers have been obliged to save for their retirement through private investment funds. The modest public pension covers only those without adequate savings.

For all its economic success, Australia is suffering from a political malaise. It used to have long-lived governments. Between 1983 and 2007, just three prime ministers held office (Bob Hawke and Paul Keating of Labor, and John Howard of the Liberals). Yet, since then, the job has changed hands six times. A full term is only three years, but the last time a prime minister survived in office for a whole term was 2004–07. For those who consider Australia's unequalled economic performance the result, at least in part, of far-sighted decisions made 30 years ago, its choppy politics seem like a harbinger of decline.

Criminal activity: law and justice around the globe

Why support for the death penalty is rising again in America

Ruben Gutierrez is in many ways typical of the thousands of people who sit on death row in America. The 41-year-old has been there for two decades. He insists on his innocence and has been fighting for DNA testing that will, he hopes, prove his innocence. He was scheduled to die in Huntsville State Penitentiary in Huntsville, Texas, by lethal injection on September 12th 2018, having been found guilty of the murder in 1998 of Escolastica Harrison, a trailer-park owner who kept $600,000 in cash inside her mobile home because she did not trust banks. But he was granted a stay of execution in August, just days before he was due to die, after new lawyers were appointed to represent him. The majority of Americans still approve of executing perpetrators of heinous crimes, despite the risk that an innocent person might be killed. And to the puzzlement of those who think the death penalty is on its way out, the number of supporters of capital punishment is on the increase again.

Both the number of executions and public support for the death penalty were in decline for most of the past 20 years. Texas executed 40 people in 2000, but only seven in each of 2016 and 2017. The main reason was the drop in America's murder rate, from 10.2 per 100,000 people in 1980 to 4.5 in 2014. Along with that decline has come a more recent fall in the incidence of the most heinous, first-degree murders. Moreover, every state except Alaska now gives juries the option of making sure that a murderer will never be released, by sentencing him to life without parole. At the same time, abolitionists are making an ever more forceful case. Strong evidence suggests that Texas has killed innocent men more than once since the 1970s, including Carlos Deluna and Cameron Todd Willingham, who were executed in 1989 and 2004 respectively. Other evidence suggests a strong racial bias. Over 75% of those executed were sentenced to death for killing whites, even though about half of all murder victims are black. Abolitionists' practical arguments include the exorbitant cost of executions, thanks to the lengthy appeals and retrials they occasion; the difficulty of buying poison for use in executions, from ever more reluctant pharmaceutical companies; and the problems caused when states choose new drug cocktails that may cause prisoners to suffer.

Why, then, is support for the death penalty increasing again? According to a survey released in 2018 by the Pew Research Centre, 54% of Americans back the death penalty, compared with 49% two years ago. Robert Dunham, head of the Death Penalty Information Centre, says this is related to the political rhetoric in Washington, DC. In March 2018 President Donald Trump proposed making drug dealers eligible for the death penalty, arguing that the federal government is "wasting our time" by being unwilling to execute them. Such talk may play well to a nation in the grip of the deadliest crisis of illegal-drug addiction in its history, though there is little evidence to suggest that the death penalty actually deters criminality. If the president's proposal were to come into effect, America would join some disreputable peers. According to Amnesty International, only China, Iran, Saudi Arabia and Singapore executed people for drug dealing in 2017.

Across the world, capital punishment is becoming less common and less popular than it was, and dismay over its cost, efficacy and methods are hastening its decline. It seems unlikely that America will buck the trend for long. Young people and ethnic minorities, in particular, tend to be more opposed to the death penalty; demography is on the side of abolition. So far 19 states and the District of Columbia have discarded the death penalty. A good chunk of those that have retained it have not executed anyone in decades. Most executions are carried out in a handful of states, such as Texas, Florida and Oklahoma, and most death sentences are sought by prosecutors in just a few counties. When Americans' support for capital punishment does start to recede once again, their elected lawmakers should pay heed. Abolitionists may end up waiting longer than expected, but even in America the death penalty's days are surely numbered.

Why Supreme Court justices serve such long terms

When Justice Anthony Kennedy's 30 years on the bench ended with his retirement in July 2018 and a partisan fight began to brew in the Senate over the confirmation of his successor, Brett Kavanaugh, public attention was once again focused on a quirk of America's judiciary: the staggeringly long careers of Supreme Court justices. Article III is by far the slimmest of the constitution's articles laying out the branches of government, but the term of office it specifies for federal judges is virtually unbounded. Judges of both "the supreme and inferior courts", section 1 reads, "shall hold their offices during good behaviour". In practice, that means for life, or until the judge decides to hang up his robe.

One path off the court – impeachment – has not amounted to much. In 1804, at the suggestion of President Thomas Jefferson, the House of Representatives served Justice Samuel Chase with articles of impeachment for letting partisanship seep into his decisions. But after the Senate acquitted Chase in 1805, he carried on as justice until his death six years later. Another 14 federal judges have been impeached since 1789; eight have been removed from office. But no Supreme Court justice has ever been ousted for bad behaviour. With Americans living more than twice as long as they did 150 years ago, a life term means that justices typically count their stints in decades. In 2006 two law professors, Steven Calabresi and James Lindgren, noted that justices serving before 1970 served an average of 14.9 years, while those serving after 1970 have served 26.1 years. The five most recent justices to leave the court have served an average of 27.5 years, and that includes an outlier, David Souter, who retired after a modest 18-year tenure in 2009, aged 69.

Why did the framers entrust judges with lifetime appointments, when every other democracy in the world imposes term limits, a mandatory retirement age, or both? The so-called "least dangerous branch" needed some shoring up, the founders believed. In order to exercise judgment free from shifting political winds, judges needed a strong measure of autonomy from the legislative and executive departments. For Alexander Hamilton, life tenure was just the ticket: "the best expedient which can be devised in any government" to preserve judicial independence. Without elections to stand for or worries about losing their seats, Hamilton reasoned, justices would be able to hover above the political fray and dispense justice impartially.

With the confirmation of Brett Kavanaugh promising to entrench a 50-year-and-counting conservative majority, Hamilton's lofty hopes for life tenure sound quixotic. Decisions like *Bush v Gore* (in which five Republican-appointed justices effectively gave a Republican the keys to the White House in 2000) or *Janus v AFSCME* (a case from June 2018 that dealt a blow to public-sector unions) are hard to spin as dispassionate judges faithfully interpreting the law without regard to their political predilections. Justices' tendency to retire when an ideologically friendly president is in office – as Anthony Kennedy seems to have done – only makes the court look more like a politicised institution ripe for manipulation. To allay the gaming of retirements, and to bring fresh blood to the bench a little less infrequently, Fix the Court (a non-partisan Supreme Court watchdog) has attracted scholarly support for a plan to limit justices' active service to 18 years, after which they would be eligible to sit on lower federal courts. The proposal calls for biennial appointments, or two picks per presidential term. Something along these lines might address a prescient 18th-century complaint from Brutus, an anti-Federalist writer. The constitution provides for "no power above" judges, Brutus wrote. Justices are "independent of the people, of the legislature and of every power under heaven". It's no wonder, then, that justices who shape America for decades on end come to "feel themselves independent of heaven itself".

Why opium and cocaine production has reached record highs

Production of plant-based illicit drugs has surged in recent years, according to the UN Office on Drugs and Crime (UNODC). The world's output of opium rose by 65% in 2017, reaching its highest level since records began. Of the 10,500 tonnes made that year, 9,000 came from Afghanistan, a country wracked by violent conflict and rural poverty. Global cocaine manufacturing also reached a record high in 2016 (the latest year for which data are available), rising by 25% year on year to 1,410 tonnes. More than half of this amount originated in Colombia.

The White House Office of National Drug Control Policy published estimates for production of cocaine and cultivation of coca, the raw material for cocaine, in Colombia in 2017. It said that production rose from 772 tonnes in 2016 to 921 tonnes last year. The area under cultivation increased by 11%, to 209,000 hectares. The increased cultivation of coca in Colombia defied expectations that the government's peace deal with the FARC guerrillas, who relied

High times
Global drug production, tonnes, '000

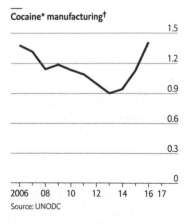

Cocaine* manufacturing†

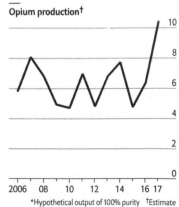

Opium production†

2006 08 10 12 14 16 17

Source: UNODC

*Hypothetical output of 100% purity   †Estimate

financially on drug trafficking, would curtail the cocaine trade. What went wrong?

One explanation is a textbook example of the law of unintended consequences. The peace agreement required the government to make payments to coca farmers who switched to growing other crops. This wound up creating a perverse incentive for people to start planting coca, so they could receive compensation later on for giving it up. The government also scaled back its aerial crop-spraying programme as peace talks progressed, which allowed cultivation to expand. As the FARC became less active, and eventually disarmed, other armed groups took over the cocaine trade.

In Afghanistan, meanwhile, poppy cultivation rose following the American invasion in 2001. After a dip around 2010, it has reached new record highs. The United States has spent more than $10bn on anti-drug efforts in the country, mainly on setting up eradication teams, giving cash to Afghan farmers to grow wheat instead of poppies and rewarding local politicians from areas where opium production fell. However, rather than reducing poppy output, this campaign seems to have merely relocated opium production to areas controlled by the Taliban – enriching the very group America has sought desperately to defeat.

Why Mexico's murder rate is soaring

In April 2018, 12,000 people marched in protest through Guadalajara, Mexico's second-biggest city, after authorities revealed that three missing film students had been dissolved in acid. The month before, a bottler for Coca-Cola shut down its operations in the state of Guerrero because of the rampant violence there. Meanwhile the morgue in the northern border town of Tijuana, where the murder rate nearly tripled in two years, was so full of bodies that residents complained about the smell. As repellent as they are, these tales are just a taste. Some 25,340 Mexicans, according to the government, were murdered in 2017, well above the previous peak of 2011. The toll for 2018 was higher still, at 28,816. Why is Mexico's murder rate rocketing?

Mexico has the misfortune to lie directly between South America's coca fields and the United States, the world's biggest drug market. The drugs trade has created criminal gangs who fight over turf and kill those who try to stop them doing business. Guns, easily purchased in the United States, flow back into Mexico. Weak law enforcement lets gangsters kill with virtual impunity. Some scholars think the rise of democracy at the end of the last century broke up truces between criminals and the ruling party, spurring more conflict and violence. As gangs wreaked havoc, Felipe Calderón, president from 2006 to 2012, sent the army to defeat them, unleashing an unprecedented wave of violence. Enrique Peña Nieto, president from 2012 to 2018, vowed to halve the murder rate – and it did drop during the first few years of his tenure.

But three new trends have brought the violence up to new levels. First, the capturing of "kingpins" has left gangs fragmented, undisciplined and prone to fighting among themselves. These fissures have helped spur the second trend: diversification. Gangs have looked beyond drug-trafficking and into activities like extortion, kidnapping and – especially – the theft of fuel from pipelines. These new lines of work are just as bloody as the old ones. The third trend, a result of the first two, has been decentralisation.

During the Calderón era, much of the killing was linked to the moving of drugs into America and was concentrated in states and cities along the border, such as Ciudad Juárez in Chihuahua. But now gangs are spreading to states which have not known widespread bloodshed, such as Quintana Roo, Guanajuato and Colima. Almost every single state has seen a rise in murders since 2015.

Andrés Manuel López Obrador, who was elected president in 2018, wants to offer amnesty to a vaguely defined cohort of criminals. "We cannot solve violence with violence," he says. But three in four Mexicans oppose the idea. The last two presidents have left behind a more violent country than they found. Few voters are confident that the current president can avoid doing the same.

Where and how most of the world's gun deaths occur

For more than 500 years guns have been responsible for meting out violence. A paper published in *JAMA*, a medical journal, by the Institute for Health Metrics and Evaluation at the University of Washington, provides perhaps the best global estimates to date of how severe that violence is. The paper finds that in 2016 alone some 250,000 people were killed by guns (the study excludes deaths from war and at the hands of police). In total, between 1990 and 2016, some 6.5m people were killed by firearms, greater than the number who succumbed to typhoid fever or alcohol-related deaths.

Shooting range
Firearms deaths by incident type, '000
2016

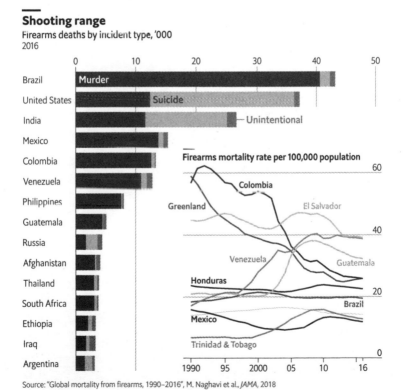

Source: "Global mortality from firearms, 1990–2016", M. Naghavi et al., *JAMA*, 2018

The data show that gun violence is extremely concentrated. Just 15 countries – representing 35% of the world's population – account for 75% of all gun deaths. India is reckoned to have suffered 26,000 gun deaths in 2016, but its firearm death rate, at 2.6 per 100,000 people, is 25% lower than the global average. Gun violence is worst in the Americas: in El Salvador, Guatemala and Venezuela, it exceeds 30 firearm deaths per 100,000 people, with the vast majority of those deaths being murders.

In 90 countries more people are killed by guns in suicides than in murders. In America, twice as many people killed themselves with a gun in 2016 than were murdered by one. Germany had fewer than 100 gun murders in 2016 but suffered from around 1,000 gun-related suicides. But it is not all grim reading. Overall, per head of population, firearm deaths are decreasing – largely because suicide is becoming less prevalent.

How horse-doping works

The best-known doper of the 21st century, the cyclist Lance Armstrong, rode on two wheels. But horses, as well as humans, can be drugged to enhance or tarnish their performance. In May 2018 eight people linked to a now-defunct racing stable in Australia were found guilty of charges related to the doping of horses over seven years from 2010. One prominent trainer, Robert Smerdon, and two of his stable hands were banned for life. They had administered illegal "top-ups" of sodium bicarbonate, better known as baking soda, which reduces the build-up of lactic acid in muscles, allowing horses to run for longer without tiring. A state authority called it the worst scandal in Australia's racing history. How exactly does horse-doping work?

Some potions, such as tranquillisers, calm highly strung horses. Others are meant to speed them up. Roman chariot racers were said to have nurtured their steeds with honeyed water. By the early 20th century, thoroughbreds were fuelled with rather stronger stuff: caffeine and cocaine. Trainers have since experimented with Viagra, energising opioids, drugs that dilate airways, and unlicensed concoctions such as "blue magic", which is thought to boost cardiovascular function. Racehorses have also been injected with EPO, the blood-doping hormone that undid Mr Armstrong, and fed cobalt, which also increases the oxygen-carrying capacity of the blood. Several trainers have been sanctioned for dosing horses with anabolic steroids, which can make them stronger and faster over the long term, not just on a race day.

Other drugs are meant to numb the aches felt by injured animals. These include exotic options such as cobra venom, which acts as a nerve-blocking agent. In 2012 trainers in America were found to be administering "frog juice", a pain suppressant 40 times more powerful than morphine, and so-called because it was traditionally drawn from the back of a South American amphibian. Vets particularly dislike this kind of cheating because lame mounts can do fatal damage to themselves and riders. In 2012 an investigation by the *New York Times* found that a rising number of horses were breaking down at American races, and alleged that doping was the cause. It noted that some tracks had introduced casino-style gambling operations, which increased the stakes and encouraged trainers to race unfit animals.

It is difficult to tell how widespread these misdemeanours are, because testing is far from universal. Some drugs, like EPO, are hard to spot, because they disappear quickly from the system. As in any sport, regulators must play catch-up with crooked chemists; and in some places, they are accused of weak enforcement. Yet their powers have grown in recent years, allowing them to surprise trainers with tests at stables. Their scientific armoury has expanded, too. Using hair samples, labs can identify illegal substances which disappear quickly from blood and urine. Scientists in several countries are developing equine "biological passports", similar to those used by human athletes. Scott Stanley of the University of California, Davis, says that by identifying abnormalities, regulators could apply further tests to suspicious stables. He believes that doping in horse racing is no longer "as rampant as a lot of people believe". Still, with cash and credibility at stake, unscrupulous players will game the system. That much, you can bet on.

What is Interpol?

It could be the plot of a thriller movie. Shortly after landing in China, the head of an international crime-fighting organisation sends a knife emoji to his wife. Minutes later, he disappears. In the following weeks, a Russian with ties to an authoritarian regime comes tantalisingly close to taking control of the organisation, raising concerns around the globe. Is this fiction? No, it's Interpol. But what does it do, and why has it been engulfed by so much controversy?

Founded in 1923, Interpol is an international police organisation made up of 194 member countries. It is not a police force in the traditional sense – its agents are not able to arrest criminals. Instead, it is more of an information-sharing network, providing a way for national police forces to co-operate effectively in order to tackle international crime ranging from human trafficking and terrorism to money-laundering and illegal art-dealing. The organisation, based in France, operates centralised criminal databases that contain fingerprint records, DNA samples and stolen documents: a treasure trove so valuable that police consulted it 146 times every second in 2017. Interpol's other main function is to issue notices: alerts to member states for missing or wanted persons. The best-known of these is the "Red Notice", a notification that a member state would like someone arrested. States are not obliged to follow these notices, but will often treat them as a warrant for someone's arrest and extradition. "Diffusions", which can be issued with less bureaucracy, are another popular way of seeking arrests through Interpol.

Notices and diffusions lay at the heart of the organisation's turmoil in late 2018. Though Interpol's constitution explicitly forbids any activities of a political character, activists accuse it of failing to enforce this rule. Much of the ire is directed at Russia, which has issued notices and diffusions for the arrest of Kremlin opponents. Bill Browder, an American-born financier who made his fortune in Russia before falling out with the Kremlin and mounting a global lobbying campaign against Vladimir Putin, was briefly detained in Spain in May 2018 after one such request from Russia. He claims this has happened multiple times. International groups have also accused China, Iran, Turkey and Tunisia, among others, of abusing the Interpol notice system for authoritarian ends. This has included the issuing of Red Notices for the arrest of refugees, on behalf of the country from which they are fleeing. Interpol often requests the eventual removal of such notices, but cannot ensure this happens.

The anger towards Interpol reached fever pitch in November 2018 when Aleksandr Prokopchuk, a Russian with close links to Mr Putin's regime, was expected to be elected president of the organisation. Critics rather overstated their case in claiming that this would be handing Mr Putin complete control of Interpol, with British MPs going so far as to recommend that Britain should find an alternative made up of "rights-respecting states". But the president oversees the big strategic and policy decisions of the organisation, even if the role is mostly ceremonial. In the end, what the Kremlin deemed to be "election meddling" worked. Mr Prokopchuk lost out to a South Korean candidate, Kim Jong Yang. But Mr Kim, who had been acting president since the arrest of the former president, Meng Hongwei, by Chinese officials, was also caught up in criticism after Interpol accepted Mr Meng's resignation letter without confirming whether it had been written under coercion from the Chinese government. Activists may have been cheered that Mr Kim beat Mr Prokopchuk in the race to succeed Mr Meng, but they continue to argue that more reform is needed. Mr Browder, for one, is campaigning to have Russia suspended from Interpol altogether.

Why "spice" is worse than other drugs

British tabloids call them "spice zombies". In America they make headlines for overdosing on "fake weed". In other countries they are users of "legal highs" who have gone too far. They are whisked to emergency rooms after collapsing or falling into a stupor, in numbers that often spike sharply for a day or two. The drugs to blame? Synthetic cannabinoids, chemicals that hit the same brain receptors as cannabis but are much more potent and addictive. They are made mostly in China, shipped as powders and sprayed onto dried plant leaves, so that they can be smoked. Spice, the collective name given to such drugs in Britain, is "one of the most severe public-health issues we have faced in decades," wrote 20 of the country's police commissioners in an open letter in 2018.

The biggest problem with spice is that its effects on users are unpredictable. One reason is the rapid turnover of the chemicals in the mix. There are several hundred known synthetic cannabinoids and new ones are relatively easy to concoct. Chinese authorities have been banning individual chemicals found in spice, but the laboratories that make them can get round the bans by tweaking the composition of their product. In addition, spraying of the chemicals can be uneven, leading to highly variable potency within the same batch. Other mis-steps can also wreak havoc. In 2017 the concentration of the chemicals in spice sold in Manchester, England suddenly jumped ten-fold, possibly because someone missed a decimal point in a mixing recipe. As a result of all this, the effects of spice and their duration can vary wildly, complicating matters for paramedics, hospitals and the police. Paranoia and psychosis are common, making some users violent.

Moreover, weaning people off spice is tougher than getting them off other drugs. For a start, some of those hooked on spice do not see themselves as addicts, thinking that it is not much more harmful than cannabis. In America, which unlike Britain has banned only some synthetic cannabinoids, such views may be partly due to spice variants being sold in shops as herbal incense.

Outreach workers who help homeless addicts face another problem. They can usually catch four or five hours of lucidity a day from a heroin addict. With spice, however, the brain is foggy all the time because addicts tend to chain-smoke it. And so far nothing makes an effective substitute, as methadone does for heroin. Treatment must therefore target withdrawal symptoms, using drugs that dull pain, stomach problems and psychosis.

For now, spice is less popular than other street drugs. In 2017–18 only 0.4% of 16- to 59-year-olds in Britain used the category of drugs that includes spice. In America, 7% of high-school students have tried spice, whereas 36% have tried cannabis. But in many cities in Britain and America spice usage has become epidemic among the homeless, who in many cases will already have drug addictions and will be tempted by something that is cheap and can apparently make the passing of two days feel like two hours. Spice is also replacing other illegal drugs among those whose careers or liberty depend on clearing a drug-screening test. Standard drug tests do not detect synthetic cannabinoids, so users of cannabis, heroin or cocaine who are in prison, on parole or in the army switch to spice to hide their habit. But the surprises that spice's chameleonic recipe can throw up make that a risky strategy.

What are *zina* laws?

Go to any women's prison in the west African country of Mauritania and you will find inmates whose only offence is to have been raped. Some are children. Often pregnant and unable to prove coercion, they find themselves branded criminals for having sex outside marriage. The reasons why are linked to cultures that routinely ignore women's testimony and to a set of Islamic laws, known as *zina*, that are enforced to different extents across the Muslim world. *Zina* is an Islamic legal term, meaning illicit sexual relations, that can be found in the Koran and the hadith (the collected words and acts of the Prophet Muhammad). Muslim empires like the Ottomans, the Mughals and the Safavids defined *zina* in different ways. But it usually refers to adultery and extramarital sex, which includes being a victim of rape.

In the past, punishments for breaking *zina* laws included whipping and even death by stoning. Now, even as much of the Muslim world becomes less conservative, abuses of *zina* laws may still incur a prison sentence and fines. The use of the laws diminished during the anti-colonial struggles of the mid-20th century because emergent states generally modelled new criminal laws on European statutes. But things changed after that. Ziba Mir-Hosseini and Vanja Hamzić of London's School of African and Oriental studies say that, thanks to the spread of Islamism across the Muslim world at the time of the Iranian revolution, the last quarter of the 20th century saw a rise in the application of *zina* laws in several Muslim-majority countries.

Sometimes the laws are enshrined in state law. Sometimes they are enforced by the community, or even by the family, in the form of honour killings. In Iran, after the 1979 revolution, *zina* was codified in particularly brutal terms, with detailed descriptions of how men and women should be punished for *zina* offences. In Pakistan, such laws were introduced in 1979 as part of the re-Islamisation of the country by the military ruler, Zia-ul-Haq. Sex outside marriage was to be considered a crime against the state. According to a local lawyer, Zafar Iqbal Kalanauri, thousands of Pakistani rape victims ended up in jail as a result.

All too often the laws hit vulnerable women the hardest. In some Gulf states like Kuwait and Qatar, hundreds of female migrant workers have been punished and imprisoned for *zina* offences. Often their "crime" is to have been raped by their employers. Sometimes the laws are enforced by conservative provinces that choose to defy reformers in the capital. In Indonesia's westerly Aceh province, for example, unmarried people may be whipped for showing signs of affection in public. According to a survey by the Mauritanian Association for the Health of the Mother and Child, an NGO, 40% of female prisoners in the country are in jail for having sex outside wedlock. Many victims do not report being raped for fear of being punished. The rapists do not always avoid punishment, but it is easier for them to deny guilt. Turkey shelved an attempt to reintroduce *zina*-inspired anti-adultery and extramarital sex laws when it tried to join the European Union. But local reports say that President Recep Tayyip Erdogan is reconsidering introducing a *zina*-inspired anti-adultery law to appease his conservative voter base.

What is an undeclared intelligence officer?

On March 14th 2018 Britain expelled 23 "undeclared intelligence officers" from Russia's embassy in London. The move came after a former Russian spy, Sergei Skripal, and his daughter were poisoned with a nerve agent in the English city of Salisbury. In a co-ordinated show of solidarity, on March 26th America expelled 60 such undeclared spooks. Other British allies, such as Australia and Canada, made similar expulsions. Who are all these undeclared intelligence officers and, if Britain knew who they were, why did it not kick them out sooner?

There are two types of intelligence officers abroad. The first are "declared": people who officially work in that role, within their home country's embassy. Almost all countries send such people abroad to act as a liaison between their own intelligence service and that of their host country, for instance in co-operation against terrorism. Host countries are aware of their identity and keep them under constant surveillance. The second type of intelligence officer is "undeclared". These people are also common in embassies but are not accredited as intelligence officers, because their official job is doing something else, for instance in the consular, political or economic section. As they are not declared intelligence officers, they are theoretically under less surveillance and can do more to gather intelligence. There are, in addition, covert agents embedded in society outside the embassy.

Host countries often turn a blind eye to undeclared intelligence officers within embassies. They will have their own spooks in their embassies abroad, and it is accepted that if you expel such officers, your diplomats and spooks will in turn be expelled, as indeed happened on March 17th when Russia kicked out 23 British diplomats. Host countries often have suspicions about who is a spook among the diplomats. But if a country believes that foreign agents have committed a crime, as happened with the poisoning of Mr Skripal and his daughter, the only way to punish embassy employees is to expel them, because they have full diplomatic immunity. Covert agents who are not diplomats have no such immunity and so, if they are caught, they may be charged with espionage and put on trial (or, in some countries, much worse).

Intelligence sources suggest that the number of undeclared Russian intelligence officers posted in Western countries has grown substantially in the past decade and that there are at least as many in Britain now as at the height of the cold war. In the short run, the 2018 expulsions will certainly have dented Russia's ability to gather the intelligence it wants. But in cases like these, as the Russians look to replace their expelled spooks, Western counter-espionage services must work hard to try to identify the new arrivals.

Why is the American sheriff such a polarising figure?

Joe Arpaio served 24 years as the sheriff of Maricopa county, Arizona, before losing his bid for re-election in 2016. Deeply controversial for his policies on ethnic profiling and jail conditions, Mr Arpaio was repeatedly admonished by state and federal courts, culminating in a conviction for criminal contempt of court in 2017. He was soon pardoned by President Donald Trump. Mr Arpaio then ran, unsuccessfully, in Arizona's Republican primary election for the Senate elections in 2018. Both he and Richard Mack, founder of the Constitutional Sheriffs and Peace Officers Association, are held up by right-wing anti-federalists as avatars of the power of the sheriff, a unique position in American policing and governance that has come to represent, for some people, a last bulwark against federal authority. Why is the job of sheriff such a polarising position in America?

The word sheriff comes from "shire reeve", meaning a county's chosen protector, dating back to pre-Norman times in England. After the Norman Conquest in 1066, the sheriff's role shifted to become a kind of investigator, lesser judge and jailer for those awaiting trial. Even that role dwindled across centuries, especially after the emergence of modern police forces in the 19th century. The post was taken to some British colonies, however, and, as more white settlers arrived, sheriffs saw their role grow. They were often the primary form of law enforcement in places that had few settlements and little or no policing. The sheriff came to symbolise order in the absence of other authority, and decades of film and TV westerns reinforced that view. Sheriffs are often responsible for rural areas, and the people who respect their position most are frequently those who reject federal officers' powers. Nearly all of America's 3,100 or so sheriffs attain office through direct election and have no direct executive oversight. Their only accountability is to the county's voters. They swear an oath to uphold the constitution and other laws, but each state defines the role differently. In some states, a sheriff's office functions like a police department for a county; in others, sheriffs may simply do things like manage county jails or transport prisoners.

It is this independence, lack of federal oversight and perceived closeness to the constitution that have elevated the sheriff in the eyes of right-wing activists who believe the federal government has no legitimate authority to enforce most federal laws, especially those related to taxes, guns and land use. William Porter Gale, a white-supremacist preacher, began promulgating this paramount-sheriff notion in the 1960s with a movement called Posse Comitatus, named after a now-obscure power of sheriffs to conscript the "power of the county" to seize miscreants and escaped slaves. Gale's work led in a nearly direct line to modern white-supremacist groups, and the militia movement that spawned the deadly bombing of a federal building in Oklahoma City in 1995. More recently, an outgrowth known as "sovereign citizens" believe they have individual power equal to that of government. They are responsible for several murders of police and sheriff deputies at routine traffic stops. The FBI, terrorism experts and other law-enforcement bodies view so-called sovereign citizens as the pre-eminent threat posed by domestic terrorism in America.

Although Mr Arpaio, Mr Mack and others disavow violence while maintaining their view of the sheriff as ultimate constitutional arbiter, they do not discount it. "The potential for violence is always there. But I pray it won't come to that. We don't want that," Mr Mack said in an interview in 2012 with the *Denver Post*. Though hardly mainstream, distrust of the federal government is not restricted to the fringe. The police chief of West Memphis, Arkansas, whose son, also a police officer, was shot and killed by a believer in sovereign citizenship, told the Centre for Public Integrity: "Even I agree with a lot of what they say. But law enforcement is not the enemy."

What is the GRU?

In the pantheon of Russian intelligence, the KGB is king. It fills the ranks of cinematic and literary villains, from John le Carré's spymaster Karla to the sleeper agents of *The Americans*, a TV show. But lately a different set of spies has been hogging the limelight. The GRU, the intelligence arm of Russia's armed forces, has been caught up in almost all the crises involving the country in recent years, from the annexation of Crimea, to the downing of a passenger aircraft over Ukraine, to the attempted murder of Sergei Skripal, a former spy, in the English city of Salisbury. Who are these hyperactive military spooks?

In the earliest days of the Soviet Union the Bolsheviks created a military intelligence service, settling on the name GRU (from the Russian for "Main Intelligence Directorate") in 1942. While the agency that became the KGB ("Committee for State Security") was housed in striking headquarters close to the foreign ministry, earning the label "near neighbours", the GRU became the "distant neighbours", exiled to a small, shabby house much further away. Yet by the end of the second world war, it had penetrated Britain's atom-bomb programme and over 70 American institutions. During the cold war, it cropped up at key moments. It was a GRU officer who formed a back-channel with Robert Kennedy, the president's brother and America's attorney-general, during the Cuban missile crisis in 1962. Another was at the heart of Britain's Profumo scandal a year later.

The KGB, which has since been split into the security-focused FSB and the outward-looking SVR, had the fame. But the GRU could boast of closer ties to revolutionary movements and terrorist groups, greater experience with weapons and explosives, and even tougher training for recruits. A book published in 1986 by Vladimir Rezun, a GRU defector, described a film shown to new spooks; it depicted a traitorous officer, lashed to a stretcher, being fed into a crematorium alive. Competition between the services was intense. When the KGB learnt of an audacious British operation to tap Soviet communications by digging a tunnel into East Berlin, it did not bother to tell the GRU that 25 of its telephone lines had been compromised for over a year. The rivalry was so fierce, writes Jonathan Haslam, a historian, "that operatives of the one were not even entirely safe from the protégés of the other".

The GRU was starved of funds and slashed in size after Russia's war with Georgia in 2008, when it failed to detect that Georgia had got hold of new anti-aircraft missiles. But its special forces subsequently played a pivotal role in seizing Crimea and supporting pro-Russian separatists in eastern Ukraine in 2014. GRU hackers, dubbed "Fancy Bear", ran riot in cyberspace, penetrating everything from Germany's parliament to Emmanuel Macron's campaign for the French presidency. But some of these activities proved embarrassing. In May 2018, Bellingcat, an investigative website, unmasked the name of a GRU officer involved in the downing of a Malaysian Airlines flight over Ukraine; the hapless spy had sent online shopping to the address of the GRU headquarters. Two months later, Robert Mueller, America's special counsel, exposed the names, ranks and addresses of a dozen GRU hackers who had meddled in America's 2016 elections. Such occasional mis-steps may not deter an organisation whose ethos is to take risks, but it has other reasons for worry. In recent years, it is thought to have suffered from heavy defections. Mass expulsions have decimated the ranks of Russian spies under diplomatic cover in the West, making operations harder. And Britain has hinted at cyber-attacks on GRU communications and finances. Will James Bond take on a GRU villain in his next adventure? That might signal that its stock was rising again.

Which countries lock up the most journalists?

In May 2019 Wa Lone and Kyaw Soe Oo, two Reuters journalists jailed in Myanmar, were released after being held for 17 months. Both had been investigating their government's campaign of violent repression of the country's Rohingya minority, and both were given seven-year terms for violating the Official Secrets Act – a colonial-era law that allows any government information to be classified as an official secret. Though they have now been released, the imprisonment of the two reporters highlighted a disturbing trend. In 2018, 251 journalists languished in jails as a result of doing their jobs, according to the Committee to Protect Journalists (CPJ), a New York-based NGO. It marked the third year in which at least 250 journalists were imprisoned around the world, though it was also the first decline since 2015.

The most censorious governments follow a familiar pattern of suppressing the media and locking up dissenters. Turkey, China, Egypt, Eritrea and Saudi Arabia accounted for 70% of all reporters imprisoned in 2018, mostly for infractions against the regime. Of

The penitentiary is mightier

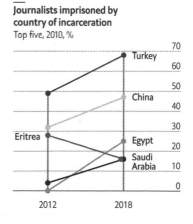

Journalists imprisoned, worldwide

Journalists imprisoned by country of incarceration
Top five, 2010, %

Source: Committee to Protect Journalists

the 172 reporters being held in those countries, 163 were detained without charge or for offences classified as "anti-state". From 2000 to 2012 the CPJ recorded a steady increase in the numbers of news staff behind bars, rising from less than 100 to over 230.

The most recent high in 2016 was mostly caused by Turkey. A government crackdown following a failed military coup suppressed and closed many media outlets. Loosely worded laws enable the Turkish government to interpret news coverage of any sort of terrorism as aiding terrorist groups. By the end of 2016, 81 reporters were being held in Turkey alone. In 2018, despite its tally falling to 68, Turkey was still the global leader for locking up journalists. All but one were being held on charges against the government. A third of them were covering sport, but Turkey still deemed their actions as critical of the authorities. Although the imprisonment of journalists on questionable charges of some sort of sedition may be distressing, the fall in incarcerations in 2018 offers hope for the future.

Medically speaking: health, death and disease

Why death is getting harder to define

When did Shalom Ouanounou die? A court in Ontario was asked to decide. The 25-year-old Canadian's doctors said September 2017, at which point they assessed that Mr Ouanounou was brain dead after a severe asthma attack, and incapable of breathing without the assistance of a ventilator. His family, though, said he died five months later, in March 2018, when his heart and breathing stopped. His case was one of several that have challenged laws governing when someone has died. So how should countries go about dealing with death?

What it means to be dead was long considered simple. A lack of pulse and breath was the standard sign. That changed in the 1950s and 1960s with advances in modern medicine. Machines could, for the first time, keep pumping blood through a person's arteries and veins, and keep aerating their lungs, after they lost the ability to do so themselves. In 1968 a committee at Harvard Medical School recommended that brain death should be the standard definition. Today most Western nations consider as dead someone who is brain dead. Brain death can be confirmed either by the end of breathing and the pulse (since someone who lacks either cannot have a functioning brain), or by a doctor's assessment that the brain has irreversibly and permanently lost its functions. There are three reasons why policymakers and most doctors have focused on the brain. One is that Western societies emphasise the importance of the mind, for which the brain is used as a proxy. The second is the cost of keeping a person on life support. The final reason is to facilitate organ transplants, because more organs can be usefully removed from someone who still has oxygen circulating in their body.

But now several cases are challenging the idea that the brain's vitality should be the key arbiter of death. Some people see practical concerns: they dispute that the brain can be called dead if some functions that it regulates, such as menstruation, continue; or they worry that people will be prematurely declared dead in order to secure organs. But the main challenges tackle the very definition itself. In many cases, this comes down to religious belief. Jews from Orthodox sects, from which Mr Ouanounou hailed, only consider someone dead when his heart and breathing cease. Some Muslims hold similar beliefs. Another case in Canada turned in part on the Christian beliefs of Taquisha McKitty, who was declared dead in 2017 after a drug overdose. Her family said that she believed that the soul is present so long as her heart beats – which it continued to do after she had been declared dead, because of medical equipment. In other cases, it is from personal or communal conviction. Japan is reluctant to see the brain-dead as having died, partly because the whole body is given prominence in Japan, rather than merely the mental part, as in the West.

A few jurisdictions have found ways to adjust to these challenges. The American state of New Jersey bans doctors from declaring someone dead on the basis of irreversible brain damage if they have reason to believe it would contravene the patient's religious convictions. In 2008 Israel introduced a brain-death standard but still allows some scope for the patient to choose (if indeed their wishes are known) between that definition and a cardio-respiratory one. New York state directs doctors to show "reasonable accommodation" not only for religious protests against the brain-death standard, but also for moral ones. Facing a severe shortage of organs, Japan in 1997 enacted a law allowing those who clearly express their wishes to be a donor to be declared dead when their brains shut down. Few dispute that, for society to function, death must be clearly defined. But challenges like Mr Ouanounou's suggest that countries should consider allowing people to opt out of their national definition – within limits – by making their wishes known in advance. Places that do this already, such as New York, have not encountered any special problems as a result, which suggests it may be feasible for other jurisdictions.

What is Disease X?

Since 2015 the World Health Organisation has released an annual list of up to ten "blueprint priority diseases" requiring immediate attention based on their epidemic potential or lack of sufficient countermeasures. The list has consistently contained now-familiar deadly viruses such as Ebola, Zika and SARS, as well as less-known diseases such as Lassa fever and Marburg virus disease. The difference in 2018 was that included among the regulars was something called Disease X. What exactly is this mysterious disease and why was it included?

The WHO's selection, known as the 2018 R&D Blueprint, was started as a response to the Ebola crisis in 2014, which infected nearly 29,000 people and killed more than 11,000. The list serves as a warning to governments that research and development needs to be an integral part of the response to epidemics. No one was ready for Ebola when it hit west Africa at that time. By listing Disease X, an undetermined disease, the WHO is acknowledging that outbreaks do not always come from an identified source and that, as it admits, "a serious international epidemic could be caused by a pathogen currently unknown to cause human disease". Experts now recognise that moving fast to find a vaccine involves creating so-called "platform technologies" in advance. These involve scientists developing recipes for vaccines that can be customised. When an outbreak happens, scientists can sequence the unique genetics of the particular virus and enter the correct sequence into the platform to create a new vaccine. In the case of Ebola, this meant an effective vaccine could be developed and tested in 12 months rather than the usual five to ten years.

Disease X could strike at any time. It could be a mutation of an already known disease, such as influenza. The infamous Spanish flu pandemic of 1918, one of the deadliest in history, infected half a billion people and killed more than 20m. Or it could be an as-yet undiscovered disease transmitted to humans from animals, like HIV, which spread from chimpanzees and has infected 70m people and killed more than 35m since 1983. Disease X could also be deliberately developed and spread by humans. Biological warfare is nothing new. In 1346 the Mongols catapulted the corpses of people who died of bubonic plague into the Crimean town of Caffa which they were besieging. In modern times 16 countries, including the United States, have had or are suspected of having biological-weapons programmes.

Despite the existence of the 1972 biological weapons convention, North Korea is believed to be not only in possession of 13 agents, including anthrax, smallpox and the plague, but also capable of weaponising them. In 2014 a computer captured from Islamic State jihadists was found to contain instructions on how to use plague, gleaned from infected animals, as a weapon of mass destruction. The poisoning of a former Russian spy in the English city of Salisbury revealed a woeful under-investment in chemical and biological warfare defence-preparedness. In 2002 America's then defence secretary, Donald Rumsfeld, was derided for his talk of "known unknowns". Today, one of them is called Disease X – and no one is laughing about it.

Why STDs are on the rise in America

Even as headline writers have spent recent years bemoaning the supposed demise of sex among the young, the incidence of sexually transmitted diseases (STDs) has surged in America. Between 2000 and 2016 – the latest year for which data are available – rates of chlamydia rose by 98%. Rates of syphilis, which public-health researchers once thought was on the cusp of eradication, have risen fourfold. Rates for gonorrhoea dropped 24% between 2000 and 2009, but have risen by 48% since then, more than reversing the previous fall.

The underlying science of STD transmission is unchanging and uncomplicated: it requires unprotected sex with an infected person. People today, it appears, are simply less worried about the risks. Among heterosexual couplings, this can be partially explained by the increased use of long-term contraceptives, like IUDs, which have reduced the risk of unintended pregnancy. Liberated from the fear of getting pregnant, the young have felt inspired to ditch the rubbers. Unsurprisingly they account for a disproportionate share of new infections. But there has also been trouble for frisky pensioners who, less concerned with reproductive mishaps, have thrown caution to the wind. In the past decade, rates of gonorrhoea for Americans older than 65 have increased by 73%.

Some of the increase in STDs has also come from gay and bisexual men. Although a relatively small share of the population, they accounted for 81% of male syphilis cases in 2016, according to the Centres for Disease Control and Prevention. As with heterosexuals, this seems to be because sex is now seen as less risky. That in turn is due to the advent of PrEP, a prophylactic drug cocktail that gay men can take to greatly reduce the risk of getting HIV. The reduced risk of catching HIV – along with the fact that a positive diagnosis is no longer a death sentence – seems to have encouraged men to drop their guard. A study of gay and bisexual men published in the *Lancet*, a medical journal, found that as more began taking PrEP, rates of consistent condom usage dropped from 46% to 31%. Other studies have shown that uptake of PrEP is strongly associated with increased rates of STD infection.

All this shows that changing sexual mores, and a reduced fear of the risks of unprotected sex, seem to be at fault – especially because the problem is not limited to America. England experienced a 20% increase in syphilis diagnoses in 2017 and a 22% increase in gonorrhoea diagnoses. Other countries in western Europe have seen even worse increases, sometimes exceeding 50%. Dwindling public spending on STD prevention – which has fallen by 40% in real terms since 2003 in America – is not helping matters. The chief methods of prevention – abstinence and condoms – are tried and true. Should these options seem too chaste or chaffing, then prospective partners ought to get an STD test (especially since most infections can be cleared up with a simple course of antibiotics). Verified testing is vital because verbal assurances, especially on the cusp of a liaison, can be misleading.

The link between cultural participation and well-being in later life

Book Club, a film released in 2018, is a parable about the virtues of reading in old age. Its four protagonists are women in their 70s who are stuck in personal and professional ruts, variously bereaved, lonely or regretful. That is, until one of the ladies brings *Fifty Shades of Grey* to their monthly literary meeting. The saucy story proves stimulating, encouraging the women to pursue enthusiastically whatever it is that is missing from their lives.

In reality, few book clubs are quite so invigorating. But the sentiment of the film – that participating in cultural or creative activities can lead to a greater sense of fulfilment in later life – is exactly right. Age UK, a British charity, has created an index of well-being based on survey data for 15,000 Britons older than 60. Its researchers found that a set of 40 social and economic indicators are the most useful for estimating a person's overall quality of life. They did so using a statistical technique called structural-equation modelling, which examines the relationship between a diverse

---

Mature content
Activities Britons over 60 have participated in during the last year, % of total
By those in ● bottom 20% ● top 20% of Well-being Index

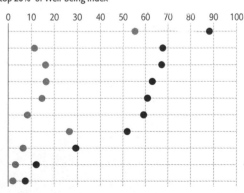

Source: Age UK

set of variables and assigns a weight to each one. The final well-being scores that the index produced for each person were closely correlated with their perceptions of life satisfaction, measured as part of the same survey. (The model excluded that survey question because the statisticians wanted to come up with an objective measurement of quality of life.)

Unsurprisingly, the charity found that wealth, health, education and emotional support all had significant effects on well-being. However, the factor with the biggest impact, when holding all others constant, was the number of creative and cultural activities in which somebody participates. The data could not reveal which type of art provided the greatest boost. Rather, the survey shows that sampling a range of activities, from photography to playing a musical instrument, was strongly correlated with a greater quality of life. Age UK's research suggests that such activities can give people fulfilment, entertainment and social contacts that might otherwise be missing in their daily lives.

The top 20% of survey respondents in terms of well-being were considerably more engaged in artsy hobbies than those in the bottom 20%. They were four times as likely to have attended a play in the last year, and seven times more likely to have visited an art exhibition. Age UK suggests that improving transport links, arranging more age-friendly events at cultural establishments and encouraging older people to get involved in the arts (perhaps at the suggestion of doctors and carers, or through advertisements in local shops) could help close those gaps. If nothing else, the erotic novels of E.L. James are at least easy to acquire.

Why Americans are sleeping longer than they used to

America's Centres for Disease Control and Prevention, the country's health watchdog, declared sleep deprivation a national epidemic in 2014. It deems seven hours of shut-eye a day necessary to function normally, and worries that few people get a sufficient amount. Data released in July 2018 by the Bureau of Labour Statistics show that, as a whole, the country appears to be getting more rest. The agency asked a representative sample of some 25,000 Americans to log and time every activity during the course of their day. The resulting data demonstrate that from 2003 to 2017 the amount of sleep increased by a minute each year, on average. The average American now rests for eight hours and 48 minutes per night.

Some of this increase is probably the result of an ageing population: the average American was two years older in 2017 than in 2003. When plotted against age, sleep patterns form a U-shape: the old and young sleep the most and the middle-aged sleep the least. That drop is steeper for men. By their mid-30s, men get

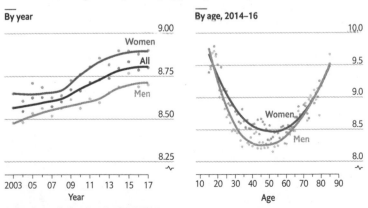

X, y and zzz
United States, average hours spent sleeping per day

By year

By age, 2014–16

Sources: Bureau of Labour Statistics; IPUMS; *The Economist*

about 15 minutes less sleep than women do, whereas in the 70s the averages for both sexes were identical. But like many things in the United States, inequality in sleep is vast. Encouragingly, about half of Americans get what can be considered a good night's sleep: between eight and ten hours. One-eighth of Americans get less than seven hours' sleep per night, but a similar proportion sleep for more than 11 hours every night.

Smartphones and the rise in loneliness among the young

Doctors and policymakers in the rich world are increasingly worried about loneliness. Researchers define loneliness as perceived social isolation: a feeling of not having the number of social contacts one would like. To find out how many people feel this way, *The Economist* and the Kaiser Family Foundation (KFF), an American non-profit group focused on health, surveyed nationally representative samples of people in three rich countries. The study found that over 9% of adults in Japan, 22% in America and 23% in Britain always or often feel lonely, or lack companionship, or else feel left out or isolated.

One villain in the contemporary debate is technology. Smartphones and social media are blamed for a rise in loneliness in young people. This is plausible. Data from the OECD, a club of mostly rich countries, suggest that in nearly every member country the share of 15-year-olds saying that they feel lonely at school rose between 2003 and 2015. The smartphone makes an easy scapegoat.

Only the lonely
April–June 2018, % responding

Share of people saying they always/often feel lonely, left out or isolated, and whether this is a problem

"Is your loneliness made better or worse by social media?", respondents reporting loneliness/social isolation

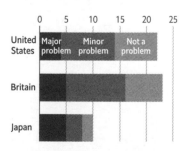

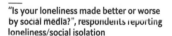

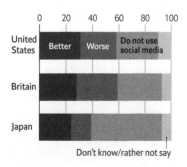

Sources: Kaiser Family Foundation; *The Economist*

A sharp drop in how often American teenagers go out without their parents began in 2009, around the time when mobile phones became ubiquitous. Rather than meet up as often in person, so the story goes, young people are connecting online.

But this need not make them lonelier. Snapchat and Instagram may help them feel more connected with friends. Of those who said they felt lonely in the KFF/*Economist* survey, roughly as many found social media helpful as thought it made them feel worse. Some psychologists say that scrolling through others' carefully curated photos can make people feel lonely and that they are missing out. It is not clear whether heavy social-media use leads to loneliness, or vice versa. The most rigorous recent study of British adolescents' social-media use, published by Andrew Przybylski and Netta Weinstein in 2017, found no link between "moderate" smartphone use and measures of well-being. They found evidence to support their "digital Goldilocks hypothesis": neither too little nor too much screen time is probably best.

What is resignation syndrome?

Roughly 800 "boat people" live on the tiny Pacific island of Nauru under "Operation Sovereign Borders", Australia's policy of exiling to offshore-processing centres those asylum-seekers who try to reach the country by boat. In its 11 months on the island, Médecins Sans Frontières (MSF), a charity, counted 78 refugees or asylum-seekers who had attempted suicide or self-harm, or thought about it. But in October 2018 Nauru's government banned MSF from providing mental-health services on the island, claiming it could do the job itself (and later accusing the charity of harbouring a "political agenda against the offshore-processing policy"). Banished psychiatrists feared the decision would cost lives. They were particularly worried about traumatic withdrawal syndrome, also known as resignation syndrome, which has appeared among child detainees. What is it?

Little is known about the psychological condition. It affects mostly children, who first exhibit symptoms of depression and then withdraw from others. Eventually they stop walking, eating and talking, and grow incontinent. In the worst cases, they slip into a state of seeming unconsciousness and fail to respond to pain or other stimuli. In Sweden hundreds of migrant children, facing the possibility of deportation, have been diagnosed since the 1990s. Some remain inert for years. Practically no cases have been documented anywhere else. It is unclear, for example, why there have been no signs of the syndrome among migrants at Australia's other foreign detention centres. Cases which resembled resignation syndrome were recorded in Nazi concentration camps, though they were never formally identified as such.

Doctors view the syndrome as a reaction to stress and a sense of hopelessness. This goes some way towards explaining its appearance on Nauru, where some "boat people" have been confined for five years as part of a process of indefinite detention that the UN has ruled illegal. Australia refuses to accept even those whose refugee claims have been approved, and seeks instead to place them in other countries. MSF refuses to say how many of the children on Nauru may be suffering from resignation syndrome. A report published in August 2018 suggested there were at least 30. The National Justice Project, a legal centre, brought 35 children from Nauru in 2018. It estimates that seven were suffering from "traumatic refusal", another term for the syndrome. Three, it says, were psychotic.

Sweden's experience raises concerns about contagion. Researchers there hypothesise that the ailment is fanned by cultural conditions: children may learn that dissociation is a way to deal with trauma. Nauru's hospital is ill-equipped to deal with the litany of mental-health problems already affecting asylum-seekers. It has only one psychiatrist, who does not speak English, and no beds are available for suicidal patients. Beth O'Connor, an MSF doctor booted off the island, sees "no therapeutic solution" for those held there indefinitely. In October 2018 a handful of conservative Australian politicians broke ranks, calling for all children to be removed from Nauru (and indeed all those referred for clinical treatment have now been taken away). In February 2019 a bill was passed giving doctors more say in the process by which asylum-seekers can be medically evacuated to the mainland for treatment. Yet there will be no end to the policy that is causing the crisis. Both of Australia's major parties support "Operation Sovereign Borders", claiming it stops more asylum-seekers dying at sea.

How genetic engineering could wipe out malaria

Gene drives are, at heart, a particularly selfish sort of gene. Most animals have two copies of most of their genes, one on the set of chromosomes they got from their mother, one on those from their father. But they put only one version of each gene – either the maternal one or the paternal one, at random – into each of their own gametes (sperm or eggs). Some genes, though, seek to subvert this randomisation in order to get into more than 50% of the gametes, and thus more than 50% of the next generation.

In 1960 George Craig, an American entomologist, suggested that such subversive genes might provide a way of controlling the populations of disease-carrying mosquitoes, for example by making them more likely to have male offspring than female ones. In 2003 Austin Burt, at Imperial College in London, described how a gene drive that could cut a place for itself in a chromosome and copy itself into the resulting gap could, in the right circumstances, drive a species to extinction.

It was a fascinating idea, but one hard to put into practice

Drive-by killing
How gene drives can quickly change whole populations

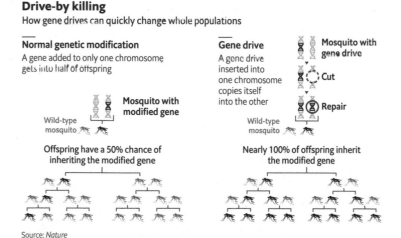

Normal genetic modification
A gene added to only one chromosome gets into half of offspring

Wild-type mosquito — Mosquito with modified gene

Offspring have a 50% chance of inheriting the modified gene

Gene drive
A gene drive inserted into one chromosome copies itself into the other

Mosquito with gene drive
Cut
Repair

Wild-type mosquito

Nearly 100% of offspring inherit the modified gene

Source: *Nature*

– until, in 2012, a powerful new gene-editing tool called CRISPR-Cas9 became available. Gene drives based on CRISPR-Cas9 could easily be engineered to target specific bits of the chromosome and insert themselves seamlessly into the gap, thus ensuring that every gamete gets a copy. By 2016, gene drives had been created in yeast, fruit flies and two species of mosquito. In work published in the journal *Nature Biotechnology* in September 2018, Andrea Crisanti, Mr Burt and colleagues at Imperial College showed that one of their gene drives could drive a small, caged population of the mosquito *Anopheles gambiae* to extinction – the first time a gene drive had shown itself capable of doing this. Releasing gene drives into the wild is controversial. So the next step will be to try this in a larger caged population.

Why was the flu of 1918 so deadly?

The flu pandemic that was first noted in 1918 was probably the worst catastrophe of the 20th century, if not of any century. The virus that caused it infected 500m people, more than a quarter of all those on Earth at the time, and killed between 50m and 100m. By 1921, when the pandemic finally receded, it had reduced humanity by between 2.5% and 5%. By comparison, the first world war killed roughly 17m people, and the second, around 60m people. Why was the 1918 flu so lethal?

It is a conundrum that scientists have deliberated over for a century, because the 1918 flu is an anomaly in the annals of flu pandemics. There have been an estimated 15 pandemics in the past 500 years, but the numbers of sick and dead were not collected systematically until the late 19th century. Of the five flu pandemics that have been recorded since 1889, none besides the 1918 episode killed more than 2m people. In an average flu pandemic, 0.1% of those who fall sick go on to die, essentially of severe respiratory distress. In 1918, that number was 5–10%.

There are two broad schools of thought about what made 1918 exceptional. The first, to which several lines of evidence point, is that the virus was inherently more potent. The genome of the 1918 flu virus was sequenced in 2005, after a preserved specimen was extracted from victims buried in Alaskan graves. It was then brought back to life. Using this, Aartjan te Velthuis, a virologist at the University of Cambridge, and colleagues have shown that, in the imperfect process of copying its genetic material or RNA, the 1918 flu virus – like the dangerous H5N1 avian-flu virus that is circulating in birds and can also infect humans – produces significantly more RNA fragments, or mini RNAs, than mild seasonal flu viruses. These mini RNAs bind to a human receptor known as RIG-I that triggers an immune response. The more mini RNAs, the stronger that response, and the more marked the resulting inflammation. Both the 1918 virus and H5N1 are known to produce massively inflamed lungs: there is debate as to whether it was the virus itself or the immune response it provoked that caused so many deaths in 1918.

The second theory considers factors extrinsic to the virus, such as the state of the world into which it erupted. According to Paul Ewald, an evolutionary biologist at the University of Louisville in Kentucky, for example, it is no coincidence that the most lethal flu pandemic on record coincided with a world war. In evolutionary terms, the optimal strategy for a virus transmitted directly between people, such as the flu, is to moderate its virulence, thereby keeping its host alive long enough to infect as many new hosts as possible. The war may have interfered with that process, though. On the Western Front, life in the trenches effectively immobilised large numbers of young men for days and weeks on end. In those circumstances, Dr Ewald argues, the pressure on the virus to reduce its virulence was relieved. The two schools of thought are by no means mutually exclusive. One lesson that can usefully be learned from 1918 would be that sometimes the worst consequences of war are unforeseen, and might come in the form of lethal, globe-encompassing disease.

What is vaccine-derived polio?

As the world enters the final stretch of a 30-year global campaign to wipe out polio, a new worry has emerged: vaccine-derived cases of the crippling disease. Such cases are extremely rare, but are attracting more notice as those caused by the wild virus itself have dwindled. In 2017 cases caused by vaccine-derived viruses overtook those caused by the wild version for the first time. The tally for 2018 showed a dramatic swing: 98 cases of vaccine-derived polio against 29 cases of the wild version. So what exactly is vaccine-derived polio?

Polio vaccines come in two forms. The injectable version, used in rich countries, contains dead viruses and creates antibodies in the blood. Someone vaccinated with it who ingests the wild virus (say, by drinking contaminated water) is protected from the disease. But, for several weeks afterwards, the wild virus in that person's gut can still be passed on to people who are not immune. The oral vaccine, by contrast, contains weakened live virus. Because the antibodies it creates take up residence in the gut, they battle there with any wild virus a vaccinated person might ingest, making further transmission less likely. The oral vaccine is therefore a better option in places, such as poor countries, where wild polio viruses are common and vaccination rates are low. Moreover, someone vaccinated with the oral vaccine excretes the weakened form of the virus for a couple of weeks. Anyone who comes into contact with this excreted virus also gains immunity, and can pass it on to others who are not immune. This sort of passive vaccination is a boon – but only up to a point. As the weakened virus from the vaccine jumps from one unvaccinated person to another, the chances increase that something will go wrong. Along the way, the virus mutates and, after a year or so, it can turn into a paralysing form that resembles the wild virus: a vaccine-derived form of polio.

Of the three strains in which poliovirus exists, type 2 is most adept at this trick. It causes more than 90% of paralytic polio cases from mutated oral-vaccine strains. So when, in 2015, the wild type 2 poliovirus was declared eradicated, it made sense to stop vaccinating people against it. In 2016, in a co-ordinated switch that took place over the course of two weeks, 155 countries replaced their stocks of oral polio vaccine containing all three strains with a version that did not include the type 2 strain. To protect people from any type 2 vaccine-derived virus still circulating, the injectable vaccine was added to routine immunisation schedules in these countries. But gaps in vaccination coverage have prevented such type 2 mutations from dying out. In 2018 they caused cases of paralytic polio in the Democratic Republic of Congo, Nigeria, Niger and Somalia. Genomic analysis of the strains involved showed that they had crossed borders, which is rare for vaccine-derived polio strains, and that some had circulated undetected for as long as four years. Health officials worry that the outbreaks may spread to neighbouring countries.

That is a setback for Africa. The last person on the continent paralysed by the wild polio virus was a Nigerian child who contracted the disease in 2016, so Africa has probably already eradicated the wild form of the virus. This leaves Afghanistan and Pakistan as its last two strongholds. But the outbreaks of vaccine-derived cases are a sign that polio's last stand may be more drawn out than even pessimists expected. When wild polio virus disappears, the oral vaccine will be replaced with the injectable vaccine. But how long such jabs will be needed to guard against the remnants of vaccine-derived polio is anybody's guess.

Green scene: environmental matters

Why is so much of the world's coral dying?

Roughly a fifth of all coral in the world has died since 2015. Some experts believe that there is now just half the amount of coral that was in the oceans 40 years ago. The northern third of Australia's Great Barrier Reef has lost more than a third of its coral in that time. Coral is neither a rock nor a plant, but an animal. A mound of the stuff is made up of thousands of tiny invertebrates called polyps, which can be anything from a few millimetres to several centimetres wide. The reefs it builds support entire marine ecosystems, so its decline is a major problem. What on earth is going on?

There are many causes. Litter is one problem. Debris blocks sunlight, and bits with sharp edges sometimes cut coral tissue. Plastic rubbish often collects and then spreads harmful bacteria. A study published in the journal *Science* found that nine out of ten corals observed with plastic lodged on them showed signs of disease. Silt from shoreline construction also smothers coral. Overfishing is another problem, as the removal of fish from the food chain allows the spread of large fleshy algae whose growth can crowd out coral. Such algae thrive on nutrients in sewage and farm runoff. Those pollutants also bring bacteria which can kill coral larvae as they are swimming to find a spot to settle permanently.

But the biggest reason for coral's decline is rising water temperature. Heat appears to render it more vulnerable to viruses. More importantly, warming can ruin the symbiosis between coral and its main food, the microalgae that live on and inside its tissue. In warming water, microalgae overproduce sugars and toxins. This leads coral polyps to spit them out. But the polyps need these microalgae to survive, and without them they turn white, a process known as bleaching. They can then soon die. In addition, the build-up of carbon dioxide in the atmosphere is also increasing the acidity of seawater, which makes it harder for coral to generate the calcium carbonate it needs for its skeletal structure.

Coral reefs limit shoreline erosion, reduce the destructive power of storms, and provide food and shelter for marine life that feeds millions of people. So a total collapse of coral-reef ecosystems would be very serious. Various solutions have been mooted. One involves cooling reefs by deploying large, floating shades. Another proposes pumping colder water from deeper parts of the ocean nearby. Numerous laboratories have begun selective breeding of corals to produce hardier varieties that can thrive in warmer waters. Others are trying to use genetic engineering to the same end. Some experts worry about such interference, saying that a coral created for heat tolerance might have other problems, such as a greater vulnerability to viruses. Opposition to such breeding is weakening, however. Coral needs all the help it can get.

Why aren't all commercial flights powered by sustainable fuel?

It has been more than a decade since Virgin Atlantic flew a Boeing 747 partly powered by biofuel between London and Amsterdam. It may have been something of a publicity stunt, but the airline's boss, Sir Richard Branson, called it a "vital breakthrough". Demonstrating that fuel made from coconuts and Brazilian babassu nuts could be used by commercial aircraft would spur development of "the fuels of the future", he said, and reduce aviation's carbon footprint. Yet a decade on, biofuels account for less than 1% of the 1.5bn barrels of fuel burned each year by commercial airlines. Why has the take-up been so slow?

It is not from lack of choice. The mix used in the Virgin Atlantic flight was ruled out for future flights because of the limited supply of babassu nuts and the harmful effects of diverting potential food to fuel. But scientists have since learned to mimic jet fuel using materials such as switchgrass, wood residue, municipal waste and even grease from restaurants and sewers. On any given day planes whizz across the oceans partly powered by fuel made from agricultural waste (United), carinata seeds (Qantas), forest waste (Norwegian) or used cooking oil (KLM). Two airports – Los Angeles and Oslo – include biofuels in their regular fuelling processes. Airlines reckon alternative fuels will help them keep their collective promise to cut net carbon-dioxide emissions to half of their 2005 levels by 2050.

Prices and policies stand in the way, however. Biofuels are between two and three times more expensive than conventional jet fuel because they are produced in small batches and because the oil price has dropped in the past decade. This price gap would narrow if biofuel production increased. But for that to happen there must be global agreement on technical standards, to ensure new fuels can safely keep a plane aloft, and on sustainability standards, to ensure those fuels really are better for the planet than the petroleum-based product they replace. And given that aviation is a global industry, all concerned must also agree on such things as who gets the credit for emissions reductions when a flight starts in one country and ends in another.

Technical standards are the easier part. Those set by ASTM International, a not-for-profit international standards organisation, are widely accepted in the industry. Even so, it can take years for ASTM to certify the process to be used for each different feedstock, and more feedstocks are being tried all the time. Sustainability is more complicated still. Measuring the carbon footprint associated with a new fuel is a given. But should its impact on deforestation, labour rights, food security and protecting biodiversity also be included? National and even regional rules on how to measure sustainability exist in places like America and the European Union, and the European Roundtable on Sustainable Biomaterials, an independent group that certifies biofuels, also sets standards. What is missing is a global standard that would permit planes to pick up fuel certified as sustainable in airports all over the world. The 192 member states of the International Civil Aviation Organisation, a UN agency, are trying to sort out sustainability measures before they start a carbon-offsetting and carbon-reduction scheme for aviation in 2021. But even so, biofuels are unlikely to reach 10% of fuel use within the next seven years, reckons Robert Boyd of IATA, an airline lobby group. And it will take even longer for Sir Richard's vision to be fully realised.

Why has shipping been slow to cap emissions?

In April 2018 delegates of the International Maritime Organisation (IMO), the UN agency responsible for shipping safety and pollution, announced that 170 of its members had agreed to reduce carbon emissions from shipping to no more than half of 2008 levels by 2050. Shipping in Changing Climates, a research consortium, called the deal "major progress" towards bringing shipping into line with the goals of the 2015 Paris climate agreement. But why did it take two years after Paris to reach such a deal?

Shipping and airlines were the only greenhouse-gas-emitting industries not mentioned in the Paris agreement. This was, in part, because assigning emissions is hard. To whom should you designate emissions for shipping Chinese goods, made with South Korean components, across the Pacific to American consumers? But similar problems did not stop airlines agreeing on an industry-wide limit within a year. Diplomats argue the slow progress is because any caps would affect exporters, too. If regulators move too aggressively they may reduce the competitiveness of seaborne trade. For instance, Brazil, a big exporter of iron ore to China, fears overzealous caps will drive shipping costs higher, helping its competitor, Australia, whose ores travel a quarter as far as Brazil's. And the idea of slowing vessels down to reduce emissions draws ire from countries that export perishable goods, like cherries and grapes, as Chile does.

Others fear that powerful lobbyists have hijacked the process. Transparency International, an NGO, has raised "serious concerns" about the IMO being unusually influenced, for a UN body, by corporate interests. A report by InfluenceMap, a research firm, found that at one meeting of the agency 31% of nations were represented, in part, by direct business interests. The way the IMO is structured exacerbates these problems. The IMO is funded proportionately according to the tonnage shipped under a nation's flag, so countries running "open registries", which allow any shipowners to register under their flag (sometimes known as "flags of convenience"), have disproportionate influence. Sometimes this helps those keen to limit emissions, such as the Marshall Islands, a low-lying Pacific nation, where 11% of all ships are registered and which is vociferous in its support of emissions cuts. But for the most part it works against them. Countries are beholden to ship owners, so those nations that are not about to disappear under the water themselves are often averse to any emissions cuts. Panama, where 18% of global ships are registered, supported a much less ambitious deal.

The IMO announcement also faced opposition from countries such as Saudi Arabia and America, who consistently oppose efforts to combat climate change (both refused to sign up to the IMO deal). Even with the agreed cuts, shipping, which currently accounts for almost 3% of total global carbon emissions, will probably see its share of emissions rise in coming years. Technology could help. New design standards are already reducing harmful emissions. Zero-carbon fuels are becoming available. Reducing the speed at which ships travel by 10% could reduce fuel use by almost a third. There is even talk of supplementing modern ships with new, high-tech kinds of sails. The 2018 agreement was a good start to encourage adoption of such changes. But as with many such agreements, the implementation is all.

Why Delhi is so polluted

Delhi does not have the dirtiest air in the world. According to the 2018 ranking of 4,500 cities by the World Health Organisation, that distinction goes to Kanpur, another of the north Indian towns that occupy the top 14 spots on the list. But with 25m people Delhi is far bigger than the others, so its pollution endangers more lives. Dirty air kills some 30,000 of Delhi's inhabitants a year – and that is a low estimate, some doctors say, if you take account of effects as varied as higher rates of lung cancer, diabetes, premature births and, according to recent research, even autism. Delhi's daily average level of suspended $PM_{2.5}$ – fine dust – is six times what the WHO regards as the maximum safe concentration. In winter it is even higher and in the weeks after Diwali, an autumn festival of lights (and firecrackers), it can rise above 50 times the WHO limit. Why is Delhi so polluted?

The answers are as multi-layered as the smog itself. One problem is geography. The flat, fertile plain where Delhi sits is bounded by the Himalayas, which block the movement of air. In summer, intense heat creates an updraft, lifting smog to altitudes where monsoon winds off the Indian Ocean can largely disperse it. But in winter, morning mist traps particles at ground level. There is rarely a breeze, but even so, colder air coming off the mountains creates a lid effect. Dust and smoke accumulate and hang. Where do they come from? Aside from the ordinary dustiness of a hot country that is under constant construction and has tens of millions of vehicles moving along poorly paved roads, there are the airborne effluents of coal-fired power plants, crematoria, fire-cleared rice paddies, factories and furnaces burning cheap pet coke and furnace oil, poorly tuned vehicles running on low-grade fuel, diesel-powered locomotives and generators, and cooking stoves fed by cow dung and wood.

Poverty exacerbates the challenge. It is not easy, for instance, to get farmers to use costly machines to prepare fields for planting wheat after the autumn rice harvest, instead of simply burning off the rice stubble. But policies have sometimes made things worse. Pushing for self-sufficiency in energy, successive governments have favoured coal-fired power over cleaner plants. They have also kept diesel cheaper than petrol, a vote-getting sop to farmers who run diesel tractors and pumps. The result: millions of stinky, diesel-powered vehicles fill Indian cities, after carmakers and buyers have shifted to the more "economical" fuel. Another example: faced ten years ago with a frightening fall in groundwater levels, states in north-west India's rice belt forced farmers to delay planting until well into the monsoon. The water table did stabilise. But the delay also pushed back the harvest. Now, when farmers burn rice stubble, the tail of the monsoon has already passed. With no wind to disperse it, the smoke drifts idly south-east, converging in the skies over Delhi.

Unlike Beijing, whose efforts to purge itself of smog have made impressive headway, India's capital is not run by top-down command. The city's government is not only slowed by elections, but by a structure of overlapping jurisdictions so convoluted it seems designed to fail. Even so, some progress has been made. For more than 15 years most buses, taxis and auto-rickshaws have run on natural gas. Polluting industries and coal-fired power plants have been shut down, and a project to distribute domestic cooking gas to replace solid fuels has grown. In 2018 the national government banned imports of dirtier industrial fuels, and introduced higher-octane petrol and diesel in the capital. By 2020 all new cars sold in India will have to conform to much cleaner emissions standards. State governments are pushing harder to stop farmers burning their fields. As the smog thickened dangerously again in November 2018, Delhi's own government banned lorries from entering the city and ordered a halt to construction projects. Someday, a concerted combination of such steps may actually bring blue skies back to India's capital. The question is, when?

How the bald eagle soared again

An avian stalker follows the course of a shallow river in Wisconsin. The river's edge is wooded; fish occasionally leap from the water. With a beat of its dark wings, a bald eagle glides along, its head white in the early autumn sunshine. Tourists witnessing the majestic sight might believe they are seeing something rare. They are not. The bird, America's national symbol, was driven almost to extinction in the 1960s, but its population is now soaring again. In June 2007 federal officials decided it no longer even counted as an endangered species. Its recovery is a dramatic environmental success. So what made bald eagles great again?

The eagle's fall was dramatic. By one estimate America had some 100,000 nesting pairs in 1782, when it was chosen as the national symbol because of its evident freedom and strength. (Benjamin Franklin lamented the choice, though, describing the eagle as a bird of "bad moral character ... he does not get his living honestly".) Within a century its numbers had plummeted. The reasons were various. Settlers cleared the nesting habitats and waterways that were home to waterfowl and other prey. Farmers saw the birds as destructive scavenger-predators and hunted them. (They did have some grounds for complaint: a modern farmer of free-range chickens in Georgia, for example, blames bald eagles on his property for killing stock worth millions of dollars over recent years.) And the birds were poisoned by accident, because they scavenged smaller birds that had already been filled with lead shot by hunters. By 1940 Congress noted that the eagles faced probable extinction, and passed an act that forbade people to do them any harm. By 1963 only 487 nesting pairs survived in mainland America, though Alaska had a healthier population.

By a decade or so ago, however, nearly 10,000 nesting pairs were thought to be in the contiguous United States. The national total is probably substantially higher today, though in places like Vermont, state rules still count the bird as threatened. The 1940 law no doubt helped with the recovery. Laws ordering a great expansion of protected natural areas, such as national and state parks, protected more habitat. Most important, however, was the banning of DDT. This chemical was used as a pesticide to control mosquitoes and other pests, especially in the early post-war years, and posed one of the gravest threats to the bald eagle's survival. DDT that the eagles absorbed from contaminated fish weakened the shells of their eggs and limited their reproduction (other birds, such as brown pelicans, were also affected). In 1972 the Environmental Protection Agency (EPA) banned the use of DDT, and the bird's recovery since then has been strong.

Given the threats to the actions of the EPA from Donald Trump's administration, that success is worth recalling. Nobody is seriously proposing a return to the widespread use of DDT in America, though occasional worries about mosquito-borne diseases, such as Zika or the West Nile virus, provoke questions on doing so. Getting the eagle back was a victory that Americans of any political persuasion can celebrate: it came about because officials employed a scientific approach to understanding an environmental threat, then implemented regulations to limit harm done by humans to nature. Given a president who calls climate change a "hoax", and who appears set on weakening institutions such as the EPA, the worry is that similar successes would be much harder to achieve today.

Why wildfires are in decline, despite global warming

Paradise, a small Californian town, looks like hell. Some 80–90% of its homes were incinerated by the state's deadliest-ever wildfire, which killed at least 85 people in November 2018. Measured by area burned, nine of California's ten worst recorded fires have occurred since 2000. President Donald Trump said poor forest management was the sole cause of the blaze. Scientists beg to differ. Academics John Abatzoglou and Park Williams have shown that temperature and dryness exacerbate wildfires in the western United States. Without global warming, they reckon, only half as much woodland would have burned between 1984 and 2015. America is not the only rich country in danger. Since 2016 Portugal and Greece have suffered their most lethal wildfires in history, killing more than 200 people. One study found that if global temperatures reach 3°C above pre-industrial levels, the area burned in southern Europe would double.

Yet despite the attention paid to such disasters, their rising frequency in parts of the West is an exception to the global trend. Most wildfires occur in developing countries, where they are declining. According to Niels Andela of NASA, America's space agency, the world's total area on fire fell by 24% from 1998 to 2015. The two main reasons are agriculture and stronger property rights. Two-thirds of the world's burned area is in Africa, a dry, hot continent where pastoralists have often used fire to clear land. Slash-and-burn methods remain common in parts of Asia as well. The growth of modern farming is helping to put blazes out: dividing land into pastures and fields breaks up terrain and makes it harder for infernos to spread. Settled people who have things to lose prefer fighting fires to starting them.

This trend is so robust that fire is expected to keep fizzling out. Across various scenarios of global warming and population growth, Wolfgang Knorr of Sweden's Lund University finds that the fire-reducing impact of changing land use generally outweighs the effect of rising temperature. This will save lives. Wildfires cause

A warmer climate has made wildfires in America more severe

Forest area burned v climate conditions
Western United States, 1984–2017

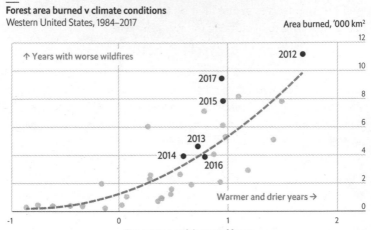

Area burned, '000 km²

↑ Years with worse wildfires

2012 ●

2017 ●

2015 ●

2013 ●
2014 ●
2016 ●

Warmer and drier years →

Temperature and dryness of forest
Standard deviations of "fuel-aridity" index, relative to 1981–2010 average

Global area burned
Using moderate scenarios for climate change and population growth†

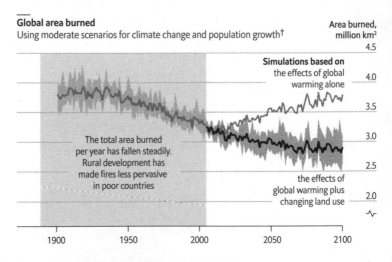

Area burned,
million km²

Simulations based on
the effects of global
warming alone

The total area burned
per year has fallen steadily.
Rural development has
made fires less pervasive
in poor countries

the effects of
global warming plus
changing land use

Sources: L. Giglio, University of Maryland; N. Andela, NASA; P. Williams,
Columbia University; W. Knorr, Lund University

*In 28km² blocks

330,000 premature deaths a year by spewing smoke, far more than by trapping and burning victims. People moving onto fire-prone land put themselves at risk. But by keeping flames in check, they make the air more breathable for everyone else.

Which countries will produce the most waste in future?

For more than two centuries since the start of the Industrial Revolution, Western economies have been built upon the premise of "take, make, dispose". But the waste this created in 20th-century Europe and America was nothing compared with the rubbish now being produced by emerging economies such as China. According to a World Bank report, in 2016 the world generated 2bn tonnes of municipal solid waste (household and commercial rubbish) – up from 1.8bn tonnes just three years earlier. That equates to 740 grams (1lb 6oz) each day for every man, woman and child on Earth.

Throwaway world

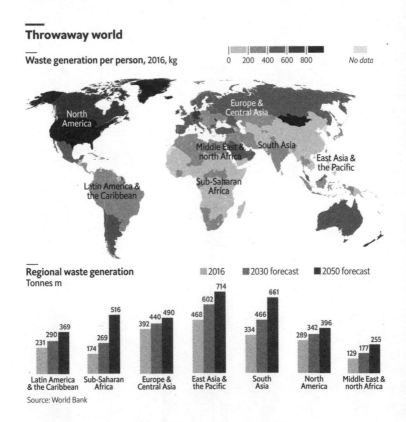

Waste generation per person, 2016, kg

0 200 400 600 800   *No data*

North America

Europe & Central Asia

Middle East & north Africa

South Asia

East Asia & the Pacific

Latin America & the Caribbean

Sub-Saharan Africa

Regional waste generation
Tonnes m

■ 2016   ■ 2030 forecast   ■ 2050 forecast

Region	2016	2030	2050
Latin America & the Caribbean	231	290	369
Sub-Saharan Africa	174	269	516
Europe & Central Asia	392	440	490
East Asia & the Pacific	468	602	714
South Asia	334	466	661
North America	289	342	396
Middle East & north Africa	129	177	255

Source: World Bank

That number does not include the much bigger amount produced by industry. Industrial solid refuse contains more valuable materials like scrap metal and has long been better managed by profit-seeking firms. And then there is the biggest waste management problem of all: 30bn tonnes of invisible but dangerous carbon dioxide dumped into the atmosphere every year.

As people grow richer, they consume – and discard – more. Advanced economies make up 16% of the world's population but produce 34% of its rubbish. The developing world is catching up fast. On current trends, the World Bank projects, by mid-century Europeans and North Americans will produce a quarter more waste than they do today. In the same period, volumes will grow by half in East Asia, they will double in South Asia and triple in sub-Saharan Africa. The annual global total will approach 3.4bn tonnes.

How modern bio-energy helps reduce global warming

Global carbon-dioxide emissions from the energy sector are on the rise again. After three years of remaining flat, they grew by 1.4% in 2017, and analysis from the International Energy Agency (IEA), the world's energy watchdog, suggests they are likely to have risen faster in 2018. This contrasts with the sharp reduction in emissions needed to meet the goals of the Paris climate agreement, which saw 197 parties agree to limit global warming to well below 2°C, and ideally 1.5°C, relative to pre-industrial temperatures. The finding came as a report by the United Nations' Intergovernmental Panel on Climate Change (IPCC), a group of leading climate scientists, reaffirmed that the world is on track to warm by 3°C by the end of the century.

Scaling up the use of renewable energy is essential to any efforts to contain global warming. Renewables have grown rapidly in recent years, and the IEA reckons this growth will continue. It predicts that renewables will account for 40% of the growth in global energy use until 2023. Renewables, including hydropower, will grow fastest in the electricity sector, accounting for 30% of total electricity generation in 2023 – encouraging news even if electricity accounts for less than 20% of global energy consumption. The use of renewables in heat and transport, which make up 80% of that consumption, remains limited. Decarbonising these sectors is essential if climate targets are to be met, but it will be impossible without the contribution of a critical, yet often overlooked source of renewable energy: modern bio-energy.

Bio-energy is traditionally associated with the burning of things like wood, charcoal and animal waste. The practice is common for cooking and heating in developing countries, but it emits harmful pollutants, and can damage the environment. Modern bio-energy, however, is different. It refers to the production of sustainable biofuels like wood pellets, ethanol, biogas (produced from the breakdown of organic matter) and biodiesel (produced from plants such as rapeseed). In 2017 modern bio-energy provided half of all renewable energy consumed – and four times as much as solar and wind combined. Biofuels can help decarbonise sectors for which other options may be scarce, by generating heat for industries and heating rooms and water in buildings, and powering the transport sector, though the role of biofuels in maritime transport and, particularly, aviation is still limited.

Bio-energy can contribute to climate-change mitigation even though, when burned, biofuels may emit more carbon dioxide per unit of energy generated than fossil fuels like coal and oil. The difference is that burning fossil fuels releases carbon that has been locked in the ground for millions of years; burning biofuels returns to the atmosphere the carbon that was recently absorbed by the plants. This is why the IEA's modelling of how to keep global warming below 2°C this century shows that the share of modern bio-energy in the world's energy mix will grow from 4.5% to 17% by 2060. Over the same period, modern bio-energy alone would be responsible for 17% of the reduction in carbon-dioxide emissions. Accelerating the deployment of bio-energy becomes even more important in light of the IPCC's report emphasising the importance of keeping global warming below 1.5°C, not 2°C, in order to avoid droughts, floods, extreme heat and poverty. Without a significant increase in investment in bio-energy and a supportive policy and regulatory environment, that goal will be out of reach.

How rainfall affected the fate of Roman emperors

During the summer of 2018 the world was stifled by exceptional temperatures. Deadly wildfires ripped through parts of the United States and Greece; Japan declared its heatwave a natural disaster; drought in Britain led to hosepipe bans and caused farmers to slaughter their cattle for lack of feedstock. As the planet warms, global heatwaves and associated droughts will become increasingly common. History offers numerous cautionary tales about the effects that these weather-related shocks can have on society and politics.

One such lesson is how drought affected the stability of the Roman empire 1,500 years ago. In a paper published in *Economics Letters*, Cornelius Christian of Brock University and Liam Elbourne of St Francis Xavier University identify a strong association between rainfall patterns and the duration in power of Roman emperors. The academics hypothesise that lower precipitation reduced crop yields, leading to food shortages and eventually starvation for soldiers stationed at the empire's frontiers. As a result, troops were more likely to stage mutinies and assassinate the emperor.

The academics combine data on assassinations – some 25 emperors were assassinated, roughly one-fifth of the total – with precipitation data collected from rainfall-sensitive oak-tree rings across the Roman frontier in France and eastern Germany. They find that a decline of one standard deviation in annual rainfall (a 20% reduction from the average) was associated with an increase of 0.11 standard deviations in the probability that an emperor would be assassinated the following year. The Gordian dynasty from 235 AD to 285 AD was particularly tumultuous: 14 of the 26 emperors who ruled were assassinated during this period. Of course, hungry troops were not the only cause of the demise of emperors. This period was also marked by plague, invasions and economic depression.

It might be easy to dismiss the lessons from 1,500 years ago. Ancient Rome had little ability to store grain for long periods or to

Reign falls

Annual rainfall and assassinations of Roman emperors, 27 BC–476 AD

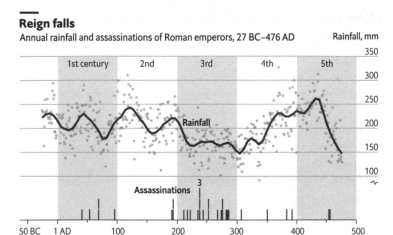

Rainfall, mm

Source: "Shocks to military support and subsequent assassinations in Ancient Rome", C. Christian and L. Elbourne, *Economics Letters*, 2018

irrigate crops. Yet, to this day, dictators rely on an obedient army to retain power. And more broadly, it has long been established that adverse weather causes economic shocks that lead to unrest, and even to civil war. For example, droughts are widely cited as a cause of civil war in Sudan, and of the rise of Boko Haram in Nigeria. In 1,500 years little has changed: extreme weather events, caused by climate change or not, tend to increase political instability.

Speaking geek: science and technology

How animals use the Earth's magnetic field to navigate

Come wintertime, thousands of garden warblers, pied flycatchers and bobolinks – all tiny songbirds – cross the equator, heading south for sunnier climes. It is an epic trip. For guidance they rely on the position of the sun and stars, as well as smells and other landmarks. They may also use the Earth's magnetic field, thanks to a sense known as magnetoreception. Theories about it have long attracted quacks. Franz Anton Mesmer, an 18th-century German doctor, argued that living things contain magnetic fluids, which, when out of balance, lead to disease. His idea of "animal magnetism" was debunked and similar ones viewed with scepticism. But magnetoreception has drawn more serious attention in the past half-century. A pioneering study in 1972 demonstrated that European robins respond to magnetic cues. The list of animals with a magnetic sense has since grown to include species in every vertebrate category, as well as certain insects and crustaceans. Some may use it simply to orient, such as blind mole rats. Others – salmon, spiny lobsters, thrush nightingales – may use it for migration and homing, alongside other sensory cues. How do they do it?

Think of the Earth's magnetic field as being shaped by a bar magnet at the centre of the planet. From the southern hemisphere, magnetic field lines curve around the globe and re-enter the planet in the northern hemisphere. A few features of the field vary predictably across the surface of the Earth. Intensity is one variable – the Earth's magnetic field is weakest at the equator and strongest at the poles. Another is inclination. The angle between the field lines and the Earth changes with latitude, so an animal migrating northwards from the equator encounters steadily steeper inclination angles on its route.

Animals can potentially derive two types of information from the geomagnetic field: the direction in which they are facing, and where they sit relative to a goal. Directional information is the more basic, as polarity lets animals orient north or south as if using a compass. But this has limited utility over long distances. A strong ocean current can sweep turtles off track; winds can do the same for migratory birds. Determining latitude relative to an end point is more useful, and magnetic cues like intensity and inclination may help. Take loggerhead sea turtles. They swim from the coasts of Florida into the North Atlantic gyre, circling it for years before returning to their natal beaches to breed. Straying from the course can have deadly consequences. One study put hatchlings in test sites that simulated the magnetic fields at three points on the outer edge of the gyre. In all three cases, the turtles reoriented to stay within its confines. Another study, published in 2018, showed that turtles nesting on far-off beaches with similar magnetic properties (like two on either side of the Florida peninsula, at similar latitudes) had more in common genetically than with those nesting closer by. Turtles, that would imply, can get lost while searching for their natal beach. They may swim to one that is farther afield but feels magnetically familiar, and breed there.

Questions still abound. The evidence for a magnetic sense is mostly behavioural; researchers have yet to find receptors for it. Part of the problem is that the cells could be located anywhere inside an animal, since magnetic fields pass freely through tissue. (By contrast, cells that enable the other senses, like sight and smell, make contact with the external environment.) Two theories of magnetoreception dominate. One says that animals have an intracellular compass. Another suggests that chemical reactions influenced by the geomagnetic field produce the sense. For researchers, this unusual ability has so far generated more questions than answers.

Why the far side of the Moon isn't dark – but is so unknown

The Moon is familiar. It is easily visible to the naked eye, impossible to miss even with the most basic telescope, and humans have stood on it several times since the 1960s. But in January 2019 China began a mission that could dramatically increase human understanding of our astronomical neighbour. Scientists will learn vastly more about the Moon's formation, and perhaps about the way in which the Earth and even other planetary masses came together billions of years ago. This mission, *Chang'e-4*, has such potential because it was the first to land a probe, and a rover, on the Moon's far side. Why can so much be learned here?

The Moon's orbit is tidally locked to the Earth, which means that it rotates once as it circles the planet. As a result, Earth-bound observers always see the Moon's same face, and observers on the Moon watch the Earth spin in a fixed position above them. Although slight eccentricities in the Moon's position relative to the Earth mean that slightly more than half its surface can be seen during the course of a year, most of the far side is never visible. (Contrary to popular belief, the far side is not always dark: its phases are simply the opposite of those seen on the visible side, so it is fully illuminated during a new moon and dark during a full moon, for example.) In 1959 the Soviet Union's *Luna 3* probe made the first circumnavigation of the Moon and beamed back the first pictures of its far side. This is how astronomers on Earth learned of one of the largest impact craters on any body in the solar system. The South Pole-Aitken basin is 2,500km across and 13km deep. Since then dozens of spacecraft have observed the near side of the Moon and six have landed people on it. The far side has been mapped, and multiple Apollo crews also saw the surface on fly-bys. In 2011 NASA's *Lunar Reconnaissance Orbiter* sent back the most detailed images to date. But all those observations of the far side have been from a distance. Until *Chang'e-4*, no craft had landed there.

What is known of the far side is intriguing. The near side is covered with *maria*, or ancient lava flows; the far side has almost none. The concentrations of chemical compounds on the two sides are noticeably different. On the near side, ancient lava flows have covered much of the oldest ground, whereas the far side's relatively untouched face has experienced billions of years of solar wind and solar exposure. Brad Tucker, an astrophysicist and cosmologist at the Australian National University, says this means missions to the far side can uncover "unique material that would be a direct snapshot of the beginnings of the Moon". One of the most popular theories about the Moon's formation is that it resulted from a collision between the Earth and a proto-planet billions of years ago; another suggests that multiple orbiting moons or a debris ring around Earth coalesced. More data from the far side will help refine or refute these theories. Dr Tucker also notes that the far side has more helium-3, a substance that is both relatively rare on Earth and excellent for rocket fuel.

The difficulty in exploring the far side stems from its position: the Moon's bulk blocks all radio signals. So in 2018 China launched a satellite to sit at the L2 Lagrange point, a locus of comparative gravitational stability where the satellite can, with some fiddling, maintain a nearly fixed position relative to the Earth and the Moon. This relay allows live remote control and data transfer to and from the lander and rover. Better understanding of the far side will affect governments' and private plans for putting people back on the Moon, for establishing stations permanently orbiting the Moon and, one day perhaps, for developing the Moon into a refuelling station for missions to Mars and beyond. "The Moon has been shown to be a giant gas station for the Solar System," says Dr Tucker. Further far-side missions might reveal where the richest deposits of fuel are.

How to collect space junk

Orbital debris offers a classic "tragedy of the commons" problem. Six decades of space launches have littered Earth orbits with derelict satellites, rocket parts and other scrap. More than 750,000 pieces are at least a centimetre wide – enough to shatter a satellite. Even flecks of paint, of which there are millions, can damage equipment, including the International Space Station. Over time, this junk breaks up into smaller pieces that become harder or even impossible to track with radar, and therefore to dodge. Mid-space collisions can be catastrophic. In 2009, for example, a defunct Russian satellite smashed into and obliterated one operated by Iridium, an American satellite-communications firm. As William Shelton, a former head of the US Air Force's Space Command, puts it, "debris begets debris".

Valuable orbits could eventually become unusable. Friction from the atmosphere in low orbits brings unpowered objects closer to Earth (their orbits "decay") but it can take many years, even centuries, before a given piece of scrap "de-orbits" by descending far enough to meet a fiery end. If, over time, the pieces of dangerous debris that de-orbit are outnumbered by those newly jettisoned in space or multiplied by impacts, the frequency of collisions will accelerate. In 1978 Donald Kessler, a scientist at NASA, warned that a chain reaction of debris-creating collisions could render whole orbits impracticable. The Kessler Syndrome, as this "collisional cascade" has become known, has probably already begun, though it is likely to unfold very slowly, over at least several decades, not mere hours as depicted in the 2013 hit film *Gravity*. Some reckon the process could be reversed if at least five big dead satellites were removed from orbit every year. (Satellites "die" when they run out of the fuel needed to keep their proper place in orbit, or lose the ability to generate power with solar panels, or suffer an electronic failure.)

An object can be de-orbited by slowing its movement, ensuring it heads rather more quickly towards the atmosphere and arrives within weeks or months. Reducing velocity by just 100-odd metres per second is often enough, though this is no easy task. As well as knocking things out of the sky, space debris could be mopped up in other ways. In September 2018 a European Union spacecraft in a low-Earth orbit used computer vision and laser range-finding to eject a net that snatched a small "cubesat", a sort of miniature satellite, that it had pushed into space. In February 2019 the spacecraft, named *RemoveDEBRIS*, achieved another first by shooting a harpoon to snag a piece of panelling brought along for the test and held at the end of a boom. A European Space Agency mission to de-orbit a big defunct satellite in 2023 has decided against nabbing it with a harpoon, and will probably opt for a net or robotic arm. The latter approach has been tested by China.

Japan's space agency, JAXA, has worked on a grappling system that would separate from a mothership and clamp onto a big piece of scrap. Interaction between Earth's magnetic field and a 700-metre steel-and-aluminium tail, dangling from the grappling mechanism, was meant to generate braking power, with the debris and grappling system eventually falling into the atmosphere together. But the system failed a test in 2017. Fuel economy would probably limit missions that seek to grab debris to removing just a few pieces of junk. That is why BBN Technologies, a subsidiary of Raytheon, an American military-technology firm, proposes using hot-air balloons to loft explosives into the upper atmosphere. A large blast there would shoot up a column of air that might slow a cloud of debris. Others have proposed zapping debris with a laser mounted on a mountaintop or spacecraft. Vapourising a bit of the object in this way would generate thrust that could slow it down. All of these approaches promise to be astonishingly expensive, but there is an additional drawback: any system that de-orbits debris could also be used to attack an adversary's satellites. So even when the technology exists to clean up space debris, the hard part will be co-ordinating its use in a way that cannot be mistaken for military action.

What are hypersonic weapons?

On December 26th 2018 a hatch at the Dombarovskiy missile base in the Ural Mountains flipped open and sent a missile streaking into the Russian sky. But the missile's warhead did not swing back down to earth with a clean, predictable arc. Instead, a re-entry vehicle detached and steered itself, unpowered, across the sky at extraordinary speed onto a target in Kamchatka, several thousand miles away. This test of Avangard, a hypersonic boost-glide weapon, was a "perfect New Year's gift for the country", said President Vladimir Putin. Russia's test highlights the early stages of what could become a hypersonic arms race between America, Russia and China, as all three countries prepare for a new era of faster, smarter and more nimble missiles. What are hypersonic weapons, and will they change the character of war?

Hypersonic weapons are those that can travel at more than five times the speed of sound, or around one mile (1.6km) per second. They come in two flavours. Hypersonic cruise missiles are powered by rockets or jets throughout their flight. They are simply faster versions of existing cruise missiles, like the Tomahawk. Hypersonic boost-glide weapons are different. They are launched into the upper atmosphere in the usual way atop existing ballistic missiles, but then release hypersonic glide vehicles (HGVs) which fly lower, faster and – to an adversary – much more unpredictably than old-fashioned re-entry vehicles. Though some, like the Avangard, are intended to carry nuclear warheads, others can use their high speed and accuracy to destroy targets with the kinetic energy of impact alone. At ten times the speed of sound, a kilogram of anything has more kinetic energy than you get from exploding a kilogram of TNT. Current ballistic weapons are very fast, but not as manoeuvrable; current cruise missiles are very manoeuvrable, but not as fast. Hypersonic cruise missiles and HGVs are novel because they fuse these qualities of speed and agility.

Russia's test of the Avangard, which followed the test of another hypersonic missile in March 2018, is likely to spur on its rivals.

China has been testing prototypes for years. America more than doubled its budget for hypersonics between 2018 and 2019, building on an earlier initiative, referred to as conventional prompt global strike, aimed at allowing it to strike anywhere on Earth in less than an hour. It hopes to field the first weapons in the early to mid-2020s, and to churn them out on a large scale. France, India, Australia and Japan are all working on hypersonic technologies of their own.

Hypersonic missiles built in large numbers could pose a serious challenge to missile defences. The low-altitude path of HGVs, combined with the curvature of the Earth, helps them hide from radar. Their speed gives adversaries less time to respond. And their manoeuvrability makes them harder to intercept. "Point" defence systems like America's Terminal High-Altitude Area Defence, which protects fixed sites from incoming missiles, might remain effective. But the unpredictable trajectory of HGVs for most of their flight allows them to hold a huge area at risk, even switching target midcourse. The technology will "completely change the balance between offence and defence", says a French official. A missile capable of travelling 1,000km at ten times the speed of sound would reduce response times to six minutes, notes a study conducted by RAND, an American global-policy think-tank. It could be mere seconds between the time the target is known for certain and the moment of impact. That could force jittery leaders to devolve control of their own weapons to military commanders or even to launch on the mere warning of an attack. And since HGVs are so much harder to spot, a large number of low-altitude satellites will have to be deployed to detect them; and those satellites, in turn, will become juicy targets in wartime. Get ready for a new hypersonic arms race.

How aircraft avoid mid-air collisions

It could have been one of the worst aviation disasters in history. In August 2017 only a last-minute intervention stopped an Air Canada aeroplane from landing on top of four planes that were lined up on a taxiway at San Francisco's airport. The incoming craft, which had mistaken the taxiway for a runway, pulled out of the landing at about 400 feet and narrowly missed the aircraft on the ground. Flyers spooked by such stories should concentrate, perhaps, on the fact that the accident did not happen. Indeed they are more likely to choke to death on a pretzel or drown in the bath than die in a plane crash. With a rate of just one fatal accident for every 16m passengers flown, 2017 was the safest year for air travel. How did it become so safe? And will it remain so in the future?

In the early 1920s aviators would fly with little navigational aid. Lost pilots would simply descend to read the signs on railway stations. Some relied on hand-signals, flags or giant concrete arrows on the ground to show them where to land. In 1935, with pilots now able to communicate through cockpit radios, the American government backed the first air-traffic control facility to regulate the skies over Newark in New Jersey. The invention of radar, just before the second world war, brought even more changes, enabling air-traffic controllers to determine the position of aircraft at all times.

The next raft of safety measures was rather more recent. Since 1993 and 2000, in America and Europe respectively, it has been mandatory for aircraft carrying 19 or more passengers to have an onboard Traffic Collision Avoidance System (TCAS). This communicates with the transponders of nearby aircraft to determine their bearing, speed, distance and relative altitude. On spotting an aeroplane that is getting too close, the TCAS issues a warning to both pilots and recommends an evasive manoeuvre, such as climbing or descending, in co-ordination with the other aircraft's system. The system, however, is prohibitively expensive for small aircraft and cannot be installed without a redesign. That spurred the development of Automatic Dependent Surveillance-Broadcast (ADS-B), a more affordable alternative that uses a satellite-based global positioning system to spot flying objects. Information about the aircraft's precise location is dispatched to the nearest air-traffic control and also to nearby aircraft.

The danger posed by other aircraft is now, arguably, trumped by that posed by drones. A report by America's Federal Aviation Administration (FAA) estimated that remote-controlled civilian drones buzz past other sorts of aircraft about 250 times every month. Although light, they are capable of harming an airliner's engine, wing or windscreen. In November 2017 a drone in Buenos Aires hit an airliner carrying 121 passengers, causing minor damage to its fuselage. Drones fitted with low-power ADS-B would be better able to avoid aeroplanes and each other. Other challenges remain. Although FAA regulations prevent drones from flying near airports, some drone operators are unaware of these rules, or deliberately ignore them. Flights at Gatwick and Heathrow airports were disrupted in December 2018 and January 2019 after drones were reported flying nearby. Military anti-drone technology has since been installed at both airports. With more than 3.1m drones shipped last year in America alone, the need to devise smarter technology and better rules to keep drones away from aeroplanes, and from each other, is growing urgent.

Why Uber's self-driving car killed a pedestrian

They are one of the most talked-about topics in technology – but lately that has been for all the wrong reasons. A series of accidents involving self-driving cars has raised questions about the safety of these futuristic new vehicles, which are being tested on public roads in several American states. In March 2018 an experimental Uber vehicle, operating in autonomous mode, struck and killed a pedestrian in Tempe, Arizona – the first fatal accident of its kind. In May 2018 America's National Transportation Safety Board (NTSB) issued its preliminary report into the crash. What caused the accident, and what does it say about the safety of autonomous vehicles (AVs) more broadly?

The computer systems that drive cars consist of three modules. The first is the perception module, which takes information from the car's sensors and identifies relevant objects nearby. The Uber car, a modified Volvo XC90, was equipped with cameras, radar and Lidar (a variant of radar that uses invisible pulses of light). Cameras can spot features such as lane markings, road signs and traffic lights. Radar measures the velocity of nearby objects. Lidar determines the shape of the car's surroundings in fine detail, even in the dark. The readings from these sensors are combined to build a model of the world, and machine-learning systems then identify nearby cars, bicycles, pedestrians and so on. The second module is the prediction module, which forecasts how each of those objects will behave in the next few seconds. Will that car change lane? Will that pedestrian step into the road? Finally, the third module uses these predictions to determine how the vehicle should respond (the so-called "driving policy"): speed up, slow down, or steer left or right.

Of these three modules, the most difficult to build is the perception module, says Sebastian Thrun, a Stanford professor who used to lead Google's autonomous-vehicle effort. The hardest things to identify, he says, are rarely seen items such as debris on the road, or plastic bags blowing across a highway. In the early days of Google's AV project, he recalls, "our perception module could not distinguish a plastic bag from a flying child." According to the NTSB report, the Uber vehicle struggled to identify Elaine Herzberg as she wheeled her bicycle across a four-lane road. Although it was dark, the car's radar and Lidar detected her six seconds before the crash. But the perception system got confused: it classified her as an unknown object, then as a vehicle and finally as a bicycle, whose path it could not predict. Just 1.3 seconds before impact, the self-driving system realised that emergency braking was needed. But the car's built-in emergency braking system had been disabled, to prevent conflict with the self-driving system; instead, a human safety operator in the vehicle is expected to brake when needed. But the safety operator, who had been looking at her smartphone, failed to brake in time. Ms Herzberg was hit by the vehicle and subsequently died of her injuries.

The cause of the accident therefore has many elements, but is ultimately a system-design failure. When its perception module gets confused, an AV should slow down. But unexpected braking can cause problems of its own: confused AVs have in the past been rear-ended (by human drivers) after slowing suddenly. Hence the delegation of responsibility for braking to human safety operators, who are there to catch the system when an accident seems imminent. In theory adding a safety operator to supervise an imperfect system ensures that the system is safe overall. But that only works if they are paying attention to the road at all times. Uber suspended all testing of its AVs and revisited its procedures. Other AV-makers, having analysed video from the Tempe accident, say their systems would have braked to avoid a collision. In the long term, AVs promise to be much safer than ordinary cars, given that 94% of accidents are caused by driver error. But right now the onus is on Uber and other AV-makers to reassure the public that they are doing everything they can to avoid accidents on the road to a safer future.

Why Python is becoming the world's leading programming language

"I certainly didn't set out to create a language that was intended for mass consumption," says Guido van Rossum, the Dutch computer scientist who devised Python, a programming language, in 1989. But nearly three decades on, his invention has overtaken almost all of its rivals and brought coding to the fingertips of people who were once baffled by it. During 2018 Americans searched for Python on Google more often than for Kim Kardashian, a reality-TV star. The number of queries has trebled since 2010, while those for other major programming languages have been flat or declining.

The language's two main advantages are its simplicity and flexibility. Its straightforward syntax and use of indented spaces make it easy to learn, read and share. Its avid practitioners, known as Pythonistas, have uploaded 145,000 software packages to an online repository. These cover everything from game development to astronomy, and can be installed and inserted into another Python program in a matter of seconds. This versatility means that the Central Intelligence Agency has used the language for hacking, Google for crawling webpages, Pixar for producing movies and Spotify for recommending songs. Some of the most popular Python packages are those that implement "machine learning", crunching large quantities of data to perform tasks like image recognition. In the fast-growing field of artificial intelligence, Python makes it easy to learn the ropes quickly, even for inexperienced programmers.

With such a rapidly growing user base and wide array of capabilities, Python might seem destined to become the lingua franca of coding, rendering all other competitors obsolete. That is unlikely, according to Grady Booch, IBM's chief software scientist, who compares programming languages to empires. Though at times a rising power might be poised for world domination, its rivals generally survive in the technical and cultural niches in which they emerged. Python will not replace C and C++, which are "lower-level options" that give the user more control over what is going on in a

Code of conduct
Ranking of programming languages*

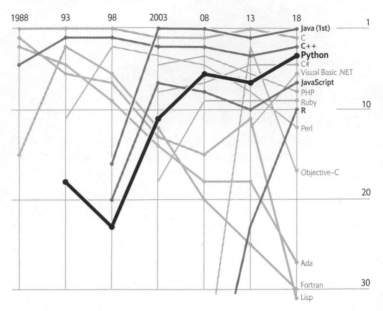

Google searches for coding languages
United States, 100 = highest annual traffic for any language

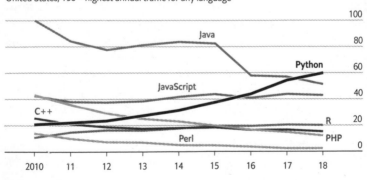

Source: TIOBE, Google Trends

*Ranked by global search–engine popularity

computer's processor. Nor will it kill off Java, which is popular for building complicated applications, or JavaScript, the language that powers most web pages.

Moreover, Pythonistas who take their language's supremacy for granted should beware. Fortran, Lisp and Ada were all highly popular languages in the 1980s and 1990s, according to the TIOBE index, which tracks coding practices among professional developers. Their use has plummeted, as more efficient options have become available. No empire, regardless of its might, can last forever.

What is "shadowbanning"?

Social networks have a problem with trolls, spammers, bots and others who degrade the quality of interaction. Some are easier to deal with: spammers have their accounts shut down. Others are trickier: what should social platforms do about real people acting in bad faith and driving away other users? Some people believe that social networks use something called a "shadowban" to partly or completely silence an account. What is shadowbanning?

The currency of social networks is attention. A shadowban, in theory, curtails the ways in which that attention may be earned without blocking a user's ability to post new messages or carry out typical actions on a network. Shadowbanned users are not told that they have been affected. They can continue to post messages, add new followers and comment on or reply to other posts. But their messages may not appear in the public feed, their replies may be suppressed and they may not show up in searches for their usernames. The only hint that such a thing is happening would be a dip in likes, favourites or shares – or an ally alerting them to their disappearance.

Shadowbanning has been in the news because of a recent debate in America. A report on Vice News observed that a number of prominent conservatives and right-wing figures in America – such as the chair of the Republican National Committee – seemed to have been demoted on Twitter: typing in the person's name in the search box didn't reveal their accounts. President Donald Trump took to Twitter to castigate the company, promising to "look into this discriminatory and illegal practice at once!" Twitter firmly denied charges that it shadowbans the users: "We do not," the company said in a statement.

It is unlikely Twitter's response will mollify those who believe that social networks express a liberal bias. A poll by the Pew Research Centre found that 85% of Republicans and those who lean Republican believe social-media sites censor political views the companies find objectionable. Facebook has attempted to sidestep these allegations by refusing to take a stance on legal speech (though it does act in the case of "inauthentic accounts", removing them altogether). Yet Facebook's algorithms must decide from millions of options what they show users in the news feed and what they hide. Certain types of media, links and text are favoured more than others. It is the absence of transparency about how such algorithms work that gives rise to conspiracy theories. Shadowbanning is one of them.

How YouTube deals with inappropriate videos

YouTube makes it clear what is prohibited on its video-sharing site: nudity, incitement to violence, threats, disclosure of private information, and so on. The company kills off accounts that post certain types of video, such as those containing violent extremism. The company uses a lighter touch, though, when dealing with lesser sins such as minor threats against individuals. These merit "Community Guidelines" strikes, an accumulation of which can lead to a ban. These made the news because in July 2018, Alex Jones, a conspiracy theorist who runs a website called Infowars, was given a strike. He then violated the terms under which he was allowed to continue using YouTube, so the company banned all the channels and videos under his control.

Every day, 600,000 hours of new video are uploaded to YouTube. The company has long had problems ensuring that new submissions violate neither company policy nor national laws. In the past, it relied on users to flag inappropriate content, which employees would then check. With complaints on the increase, the company last year began using algorithms to analyse films for their appropriateness, an approach it had previously adopted for identifying films that infringed copyright laws. YouTube removed more than 8m videos in the fourth quarter of 2017, over 85% of which were flagged by machine-learning algorithms. It now has almost 10,000 people examining videos that have been flagged up either by machines or by users (particularly members of its Trusted Flagger programme).

Videos that have been tagged and deemed inappropriate (but not so inappropriate as to necessitate the immediate closure of the account) are removed from the site and their creator is given a strike. At that point the account-holder may be prohibited from live-streaming for 90 days, as Mr Jones was. If the account-holder ignores the prohibition they may be banned altogether. (This was Mr Jones's fate after he put up a livestream on another YouTube channel under his control.) If during those 90 days they get a second strike unrelated to the first, they are stopped from posting any content at all for two weeks. A third strike sees the account deleted. Mr Jones got his strike after posting four videos that YouTube removed for violating its policies on hate speech and child endangerment. One showed a child being pushed to the ground, and another alleged that Islam had conquered Europe. Oddly, a video in which Mr Jones mimed shooting Robert Mueller, the special counsel who investigated Russian influence on the election of 2016, was not deemed offensive. Mr Jones was given a strike in February 2018 in relation to a video alleging that David Hogg, a survivor of the shooting at Stoneman Douglas High School in Florida, was an actor, but that strike had expired.

In the past, apparently concerned about accusations of liberal bias, YouTube has seemed unwilling to take action against those who run popular but controversial accounts. The three-strike system offers a way to chastise an offender and then allow them to make amends. By deciding that four offending videos by Mr Jones merited just a single strike, YouTube did little to dispel accusations of timidity. But its subsequent action in banning Mr Jones suggests that a line has been crossed. Mr Jones may have hoped that YouTube would be loath to cross a figure praised by President Donald Trump. The fact that he has now disappeared from the world's most popular video-streaming service may signal a change in the way the company deals with such accounts.

How much is Google worth to you?

One of the great riddles about the American economy is why its growth has slowed down so much during the past few decades. Between 1946 and 1975, America's GDP per person grew at an average annual rate of 2.3% a year. On average, it has grown by just 1.8% a year since.

Many economists believe that national accounts may underestimate the economic significance of technological innovations. Despite the advent of the internet, smartphones and artificial intelligence, the official value added by the information industry as a share of GDP has scarcely changed since 2000. What might explain this paradox?

Part of the problem is that GDP as a measure only takes into account goods and services that people pay money for. Internet firms like Google and Facebook do not charge consumers for access, which means that national-income statistics will underestimate how much consumers have benefited from their rise. One way to quantify how much these internet services are worth is by asking

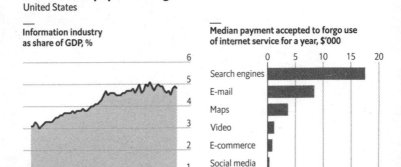

You couldn't pay me enough
United States

Information industry as share of GDP, %

Median payment accepted to forgo use of internet service for a year, $'000

Sources: "Using massive online choice experiments to measure changes in well-being", E. Brynjolfsson, F. Eggers and A. Gannamaneni, *Proceedings of the National Academy of Sciences*, 2019; Bureau of Economic Analysis

people how much money they would have to be paid to forgo using them for a year. A working paper by three economists, Erik Brynjolfsson, Felix Eggers and Avinash Gannamaneni, does exactly this and finds that the value for consumers of some internet services can be substantial. Survey respondents said that they would have to be paid $3,600 to give up internet maps for a year, and $8,400 to give up email. Search engines appear to be especially valuable: consumers surveyed said that they would have to be paid $17,500 to forgo their use for a year.

Will wearable devices make us healthier?

Apple, the giant electronics firm, activated an intriguing new feature on the latest model of its smartwatch in December 2018. The Apple Watch series 4 can perform a mobile electrocardiogram (ECG) and has thus become the first mass-consumer medical device. It is part of an effort by Apple to make its watch "a guardian of health". The ECG feature – which was launched in Europe in March 2019 – notifies users of a condition called atrial fibrillation, an irregular heartbeat that can lead to conditions such as stroke or heart failure. The watch could already tell users if they had a fast or slow heartbeat, and can call the emergency services if they fall and fail to get up.

Health- and life-insurance companies seem to think wearable devices can actually make users healthier. They are increasingly underwriting the cost of a range of wearables, including devices from Fitbit, Garmin and Polar. Aetna and UnitedHealthcare, two big American health insurers, have created a plan that subsidises the cost of Apple's pricey watch. Customers of other insurers willing to upload their movement data can obtain a discount on health or life insurance. The more active they are, the greater the financial reward. Yang Zheng, the boss of Ping An Health Insurance in Shanghai, says 1.5m customers are already uploading activity data every day. But are these efforts any more than a gimmick? Wearables have long been a bit of a joke, with some complaining that their "time to drawer" – the time it takes for people to lose interest and abandon them – can be measured in months.

Another insurance firm, the Vitality Group, set out to answer this question in 2015 when it started offering customers Apple Watches. The results of its study of 400,000 people suggest they are anything but gimmicky. Customers using the watch, along with incentives such as free coffee and cinema tickets, increased their physical activity by 34% over two years. Overweight customers showed vastly larger improvements. This represents a long-term shift in behaviour and is a big deal for insurers and governments struggling with the rise in chronic diseases such as diabetes and lung disease that is driven partly by a lack of physical activity. The key to success, it appears, is to give the watch away free, but to make users pay larger premiums if they fail to meet activity goals.

These findings could indicate a way to expand the watches' customer base. Just as mobile-network operators sometimes subsidise the cost of smartphones, insurers, employers and even governments might be willing to underwrite smart watches. There are rumours that Apple is trying to develop a glucose-monitoring function, and other features could be developed that offer an early warning of the onset of Parkinson's or monitor recovery from a disease or operation. Analysts have speculated whether the firm might add features to measure blood pressure, body fat, body temperature or blood oxygenation, and whether Airpods (Apple's wireless headphones) might be adapted to include sensors. Of course, if Apple gets things wrong, healthy people could end up going to the doctor needlessly, with concerns over harmless problems. But technology insiders say Apple is being careful and will only alert users of an issue after a number of worrying readings have been noted. If the technology of wearable devices continues to improve, then at some point in the future users may even find the doctor ringing them for information – and not the other way round.

Contributors

The editor wishes to thank the authors and data journalists who created the explainers and accompanying graphics on which this book is based:

Jack Aldwinckle, Helen Atkinson, Ryan Avent, Adam Barnes, Sarah Birke, Will Brown, Joel Budd, Slavea Chankova, Josie Delap, Agathe Demarais, Sarah Donilon, Graham Douglas, Doug Dowson, Mark Doyle, Madelaine Drohan, Emma Duncan, Celina Dunlop, Richard Ensor, Glenn Fleishman, Bo Franklin, James Fransham, Alice Fulwood, Livia Gallarati, Tom Gardner, Fred Harter, Shakeel Hashim, Alice Hearing, Melissa Heikkila, Hal Hodson, Shashank Joshi, Rachel Judah, Idrees Kahloon, Soumaya Keynes, Daniel Knowles, Krister Koskelo, Abhishek Kumar, Maximilien Lambertson, Ana Lankes, Sarah Leo, Natasha Loder, John McDermott, Dave McKelvey, Matt McLean, David McNeill, Steve Mazie, Adam Meara, Jason Palmer, Lloyd Parker, Jan Piotrowski, Simon Rabinovitch, Aman Rizvi, Adam Roberts, Max Rodenbeck, Dan Rosenheck, Marie Segger, Alex Selby-Boothroyd, Colby Smith, Joshua Spencer, Laura Spinney, Amber Stevenson, Ben Sutherland, Liam Taylor, James Tozer, Alex Travelli, Vendeline von Bredow, Kennett Werner, Eleanor Whitehead and Wade Zhou.

For more explainers and charts from *The Economist*, visit economist. com

Index